"Scharen's book  a presentation of Pi to ethnography from a theological perspective. Doing one of these would have been achievement; doing both well while having each feed the other is a double gift. It is sure to be a touchstone for theological ethnography for some time to come."

—Todd **Whitmore**, associate professor, Department of Theology, concurrent associate professor, Department of Anthropology, University of Notre Dame

"Contemporary theological work inevitably involves assumptions about the world and the people in it. We cannot avoid importing our understandings of human beings into our theology. Yet many theologians conveniently ignore this fact and rely on speculation and anecdote to accomplish their work. Fortunately, scholars like Christian Scharen acknowledge the crucial importance of adequately grasping the social world. By treating disciplined observation as a spiritual exercise, *Fieldwork in Theology* forces us to see immersion in the world not as a secular academic assignment but as a profound responsibility to discern the movement of God in our midst."

—Gerardo **Martí**, L. Richardson King Associate Professor of Sociology, Davidson College; author of *The Deconstructed Church: Understanding Emerging Christianity*

"Christian Scharen has produced a truly interdisciplinary book that models a theology rooted in the social realities of life. Combining empirical case studies and a careful, reflective approach to social theory, Scharen addresses a range of topics at the heart of both the theological enterprise and the broader human drive for meaning. A valuable contribution to ongoing debates about how theology and social science may enrich one another."

—Mathew **Guest**, reader in the sociology of religion, Durham University

THE CHURCH AND POSTMODERN CULTURE

James K. A. Smith, series editor
www.churchandpomo.org

The Church and Postmodern Culture series features high-profile theorists in continental philosophy and contemporary theology writing for a broad, nonspecialist audience interested in the impact of postmodern theory on the faith and practice of the church.

Also available in the series

Merold Westphal, *Whose Community? Which Interpretation? Philosphical Hermeneutics for the Church*

James K. A. Smith, *Who's Afraid of Postmodernism? Taking Derrida, Lyotard, and Foucault to Church*

Who's Afraid of Relativism? Community, Contingency, and Creaturehood

John D. Caputo, *What Would Jesus Deconstruct? The Good News of Postmodernism for the Church*

Carl Raschke, *GloboChrist: The Great Commission Takes a Postmodern Turn*

Graham Ward, *The Politics of Discipleship: Becoming Post-material Citizens*

Daniel M. Bell Jr., *The Economy of Desire: Christianity and Capitalism in a Postmodern World*

Bruce Ellis Benson, *Liturgy as a Way of Life*

Fieldwork in Theology

Exploring the Social Context
of God's Work in the World

Christian Scharen

Baker Academic
a division of Baker Publishing Group
Grand Rapids, Michigan

Published by Baker Academic
a division of Baker Publishing Group
P.O. Box 6287, Grand Rapids, MI 49516-6287
www.bakeracademic.com

Printed in the United States of America

Library of Congress Cataloging-in-Publication Data

Scharen, Christian, 1966–
    Fieldwork in theology : exploring the social context of God's work in the world / Christian Scharen.
        pages cm. — (The church and postmodern culture)
    Includes bibliographical references and index.
    ISBN 978-0-8010-4930-9 (pbk.)
    1. Theology—Methodology. 2. Pastoral theology—Fieldwork. 3. Bourdieu, Pierre, 1930–2002. 4. Postmoderninsm—Religious aspects—Christianity. I. Title.
BR118.S325 2015
261—dc23   2015007078

Scripture quotations are from the New Revised Standard Version of the Bible, copyright © 1989, by the Division of Christian Education of the National Council of the Churches of Christ in the United States of America. Used by permission. All rights reserved.

15 16 17 18 19 20 21   7 6 5 4 3 2 1

To Robert N. Bellah, 1927–2013
in memoriam

Contents

Series Preface

Current discussions in the church—from emergent "postmodern" congregations to mainline "missional" congregations—are increasingly grappling with philosophical and theoretical questions related to postmodernity. In fact, it could be argued that developments in postmodern theory (especially questions of "post-foundationalist" epistemologies) have contributed to the breakdown of former barriers between evangelical, mainline, and Catholic faith communities. Postliberalism—a related "effect" of postmodernism—has engendered a new, confessional ecumenism wherein we find nondenominational evangelical congregations, mainline Protestant churches, and Catholic parishes all wrestling with the challenges of postmodernism and drawing on the culture of postmodernity as an opportunity for rethinking the shape of our churches.

This context presents an exciting opportunity for contemporary philosophy and critical theory to "hit the ground," so to speak, by allowing high-level work in postmodern theory to serve the church's practice—including all the kinds of congregations and communions noted above. The goal of this series is to bring together high-profile theorists in continental philosophy and contemporary theology to write for a broad, nonspecialist audience interested in the impact of postmodern theory on the faith and practice of the church. Each book in the series will, from different angles and with different questions, undertake to answer questions such as, What does postmodern theory have to say about the shape of the church? How should concrete, in-the-pew and on-the-ground religious practices be impacted by postmodernism? What should the church look like in post-modernity? What has Paris to do with Jerusalem?

The series is ecumenical not only with respect to its ecclesial destinations but also with respect to the facets of continental philosophy and theory that are represented. A wide variety of theoretical commitments will be included, ranging from deconstruction to Radical Orthodoxy, including voices from Badiou to Žižek and the usual suspects in between (Nietz-sche, Heidegger, Levinas, Derrida, Foucault, Irigaray, Rorty, and others). Insofar as postmodernism occasions a retrieval of ancient sources, these contemporary sources will be brought into dialogue with Augustine, Irenaeus, Aquinas, and other resources. Drawing on the wisdom of established scholars in the field, the series will provide accessible introductions to postmodern thought with the specific aim of exploring its impact on ecclesial practice. The books are offered, one might say, as French lessons for the church.

Series Editor's Foreword

The Church and Postmodern Culture series was conceived and launched in the heady days of Radical Orthodoxy's braggadocio and the "emergent" church's hip humility. In both cases, French theory was invoked alongside Stanley Hauerwas to either exhort the church to "be the church" or as a catalyst to "rethink" church. In many and various ways, postmodernism turned out to be an occasion for a renewal of interest in ecclesiology. People were less and less interested in an abstract "Christianity" and more concerned with an embodied "church."

But there was a problem: this "church" turned out to be no less abstract. All kinds of beautiful, marvelous, transformative, even magical powers were attributed to this "church"—it was variously an alternative society, a haven from liberalism, an outpost of the kingdom, a community of reconciliation, and more. It sounded like another country. We couldn't wait to go there. Sign me up! What's the address? Or if you were part of the emergent crew, your goal was to "plant" this church.

So we showed up. And then the disappointment settled in. It turned out that this "church" was going to be a little harder to find. It didn't seem to exist anywhere we could find on our terrestrial maps. While all kinds of grand claims were made about this "church," we started to wonder if it only existed in John Milbank's head.

It was right around this time that I read what I consider a landmark article by Christian Scharen. Published in 2005 in the *Scottish Journal of Theology*, Scharen's essay, "'Judicious Narratives,' or Ethnography *as* Ecclesiology" was a game-changer for me. Echoing work in his first book, *Public Worship and Public Work: Character and Commitment in Local Congregational Life* (2004), Scharen pointed out the idealized nature of the church in so much of the recent enthusiasm for the formative power of "the church." As Scharen noted, a lot of folks who spent lifetimes in local congregations sure looked an awful like their neighbors who didn't. While some theologians want to deflect such "empirical" concerns with a priori provisos, Scharen's questions seemed exactly right: if you're going to make grandiose claims about "the church," isn't it fair to ask if any actual churches do what you claim? Any theology that refuses Gnosticism needs to be somehow accountable to empirical realities. As soon as I read this essay, I knew I wanted Scharen to publish a book in the Church and Postmodern Culture series.

As Scharen notes in this new book, the tempering of ecclesiological magic is only the flipside of cultivating a healthy, intentional, theologically sensitive attention to "the world." Theology *as* ethnography complicates any easy bifurcation between church and world without simply eliding the two. This is honest theology that can still be a gift to the church—or more specifically, to real, tangible, messy congregations you find down the street.

There is more than one way for theology to take the "turn to practice." If a "MacIntyrean" version of this has been centered around Hauerwas, Milbank, and others, there is an alternative stream of "practices-talk" that is more bottom-up and more appreciative of the contributions of the social sciences. Scharen's work emerges from this stream and represents a constellation of sociologically sophisticated theology one finds at Emory and Vanderbilt. (And while we tend to think of Duke Divinity School as a bastion of the MacIntyrean school, in fact we can find both schools of thought at work there, particularly in the work of Mary McClintock Fulkerson and Luke Bretherton.) While my own sympathies are with the MacIntyrean project, Scharen's convincing challenge has complicated that.

Fieldwork in Theology embodies exactly what we envisioned for this series ten years ago: "French lessons for the church." Scharen has provided an instructive primer on the influential work of Pierre Bourdieu and along the way helps us appreciate the significance of lesser known French theorists who influenced him like Gaston Bachelard. But all of this is with a view to equipping pastors as ethnographers of local contexts—and of their own congregations—in the service of mission. It's precisely why I think this book should be required reading for every doctoral program in the country and am grateful to have it as part of the Church and Postmodern Culture library.

James K. A. Smith

Preface

While the world is facing dramatic challenges—including perhaps most dramatically the crisis of global warming and its many and diverse environmental impacts—many traditional churches in North America and Europe seem stuck in a myopic focus on their own declining institutional life. If vitality is to find a way in these older traditions and emerge in new church movements, it requires looking outward to inquire how God is at work loving the world and acting for its good amid real burdens and brokenness. This looking outward is just what the craft of fieldwork in theology has in mind, and so I offer it as a tool toward "getting involved" in what God is doing in the world.

In a way, this book is the latest effort in a hope for the integration of theology and social science, a hope I gained from my first teacher in sociology, Robert N. Bellah. Titled *Fieldwork in Theology*, this book aims both to articulate such an approach and to show why it matters for understanding the church as a concrete or lived reality in and for the world. The book centers on Pierre Bourdieu, whose own academic training was in philosophy, yet he became one of the most significant social scientists of the twentieth century. In addition, his trajectory from philosophy to social science served as both prelude and impetus for a shift in theology. Whereas theology had for many centuries turned to philosophy as its main conversation partner, theology since the 1960s has experienced what Kathryn Tanner has termed a "turn to culture."[1]

In order to help make sense of his significance for theological work, the book spells out some key influences on Bourdieu's development as well as how his work takes root in one of his students, now a prominent sociologist himself. All along the way, the book tries to hold in tension the key ideas of important thinkers and the sometimes unexpectedly fruitful use such ideas might have for the church and its leadership.

At many religious studies programs, divinity schools, and theological seminaries, doctoral programs (PhD and DMin especially) increasingly require or allow their students to pursue projects including fieldwork. Such programs typically "borrow" social science methods for gathering data and then engage in theological reflection on the data. Work in theology has alternatively critiqued such "borrowing" and moved ahead with it uncritically. Recently, however, new efforts have emerged that aim to articulate an approach called "theological ethnography," or what I am here calling "fieldwork in theology." This approach has shown itself to be very attractive to students. This book has been written to serve a student audience but will hopefully also circulate among teachers and pastors generally as a practical aid in their ongoing vocation in their respective institutions.

The "theological ethnography" approach has also gained an audience among a network of scholars—both theologians and social scientists—here in the United States as well as in various countries beyond. I am glad if the book serves scholars who already, or who hope to pursue, such theological research.

1. Kathryn Tanner, *Theories of Culture: A New Agenda for Theology* (Minneapolis: Fortress, 1997); Delwin Brown, Sheila Greeve Davaney, and Kathryn Tanner, eds., *Converging on Culture: Theologians in Dialogue with Cultural Analysis and Criticism* (New York: Oxford University Press, 2001).

However, beware: those looking for a how-to book for research will not find it here. This book is in many ways a textbook about method, but it is really a preliminary discussion of what one is doing when, as part of a theological project, one does fieldwork. In that sense it is similar to Bourdieu's own book on the craft of sociology, which he subtitled *Epistemological Preliminaries*. The book is not without any practical helps for doing fieldwork, however. I discuss examples of exemplary fieldwork, and one of the best ways to learn is to carefully watch (or read about) the fieldwork projects of good practitioners of the craft.

I am conscious of the disjunction between the complexity of the material I cover and the limitations of an accessible and brief book. A desire for wide use drives my choice here regarding accessibility and brevity, and some readers will rightly want more. For them, I have included many footnotes to encourage deeper engagement. In addition, I am planning a companion volume tentatively titled *The Theo-logic of Practice*, in which I will take up the same range of issues at much greater depth.

Last, I am grateful for the support of colleagues, friends, and family along the way in my formation as a theologian and social scientist and in the process of writing this book. There are many, and I trust they know who they are and that I deeply appreciate them. One central person to my formation in social science, whom I can no longer thank personally, is my first teacher in sociology and my first coach in fieldwork, Robert N. Bellah. My years at the Graduate Theological Union and the University of California Berkeley were an intellectual watershed for me. My intellectual trajectory was set during those years, and Bellah's passion and insight were a crucial part of it. I went on to study at Emory with Bellah's student and long-time collaborator Steven M. Tipton. Steve took over where Bellah left off, taking me deeper into the great literature of Western social thought and coaching me in the craft of fieldwork. They conspired to publish *The Bellah Reader* a few years ago and

included in that volume a section on sociology and theology.[2]
This offered recent evidence of what I already knew: these two
disciplines animated the life of this brilliant scholar and church-
man, and he wrestled, unsatisfied with the disciplinary divide
holding them apart. May this little book contribute in my own
way to the rapprochement for which he hoped.

2. Robert N. Bellah and Steven M. Tipton, *The Bellah Reader* (Durham, NC:
Duke University Press, 2006), 451–522.

Fieldwork in Theology

Waking Up to the World God Loves

> Whether you've never heard the name Pierre Bourdieu or you've already read some of his highly regarded yet quite difficult writings, this chapter puts Bourdieu in context, introduces the contours of his social science, and situates it in relation to the theological challenges of the church in a secular age. First, however, a musical prelude to lead us into the chapter's main themes.

A Prelude from John Legend and The Roots: "Wake Up, Everybody"

"Wake up, everybody, no more sleeping in bed."[1] Forty years later, the urgency of this classic 1970s soul tune comes alive as

---

1. "Wake Up, Everybody," on John Legend and The Roots, *Wake Up!* (New York: Columbia, 2010). The song is a cover of Harold Melvin and the Blue Notes' 1975 song of the same name written by John Whitehead, Gene McFadden, and Victor Carstarphen and memorably sung by Teddy Pendergrass.

John Legend and Melanie Fiona's vocals soar above the funky beat laid down by The Roots. A closing guest appearance by Chicago hip-hop artist Common adds provocative rhymes. Originally written in the activist spirit of the civil rights movement of the 1960s, the song is the center of gravity for an album inspired by the 2008 United States presidential election season, when so many people engaged the political process for the first time. Despite its contemporary musical and lyrical feel, the song draws on a biblical urgency. Saint Paul, writing in Romans, echoes Jesus's summary of the law "in this word, 'Love your neighbor as yourself.' Love does no wrong to a neighbor, therefore love is the fulfilling of the law" (Rom. 13:9–10). He then appeals to his fellow Christians to "wake from sleep," for salvation is near, the night far gone, and it is time to "put on" the works of Christ in the struggle for a world healed and made new (vv. 11–12).

Under the swinging groove of bassist Owen Biddle, the verses of "Wake Up, Everybody" progressively "wake up" the people who can respond to the troubles of the world: "So much hatred, war, and poverty." First, Melanie Fiona calls out to "wake up all the teachers," who are to teach in a new way. The youngest, she croons, are our future, those whose world we are making today. Next, John Legend sounds the wake-up call for "all the doctors" to make the old people well. The latter are, he reminds us, the ones who have suffered a long road of this-worldly troubles, and they deserve to be cared for in their final years. Fiona then encourages all the builders to wake up and "build a new land." She clearly casts a wide net here: the song implies we are all builders. Common picks up the theme, trying to "write a song as sweet as the Psalms." He acknowledges the "earthquakes, wars, and rumors" but claims a powerful identity able to fund the call for renewed work for good. We are, Common pleads, "more than consumers, we're more than shooters, more than looters." Instead, we are "created in [God's] image" so that God can "live through us."

The album as a whole carries the urgency set by the title, *Wake Up!* Take the first track on the album, an intense cover of Baby Huey's 1971 soulful lament "Hard Times."[2] The picture of daily struggle is bleak: John Legend and Questlove tell us about hard times "sleepin' on motel floors / knockin' on my brother's door / eatin' Spam and Oreos and drinkin' Thunderbird, baby." Especially as a lament sung out of the African American experience, the song echoes the real-life struggles of people barely making it day to day. But in keeping with the empowerment of the times—both the activist era of the 60s and early 70s, as well as the swell of political participation in 2008—the final song of the album, "Shine," strikes a hopeful note.[3] Granted, it is a song John Legend wrote for Davis Guggenheim's film *Superman*, a film depicting the brokenness of America's public school system. Yet Guggenheim's film finds strength and hope in focusing in depth on several students, and Legend's song picks this up. "So dark, but I see sparks, if we don't snuff them out / We gotta let them flame / Let them speak their name / Let them reach up to the clouds / Let them shine." The yearning of Legend's voice and the soft intensity of the music echo the song's words in reaching for hope. Together they offer a powerful combination of hope and urgency summing up the album as a whole.

Speaking about the genesis of the album, John Legend describes how inspiring it was to watch young people during the 2008 presidential election, many empowered for the first time to join the political process and thereby seek a better world. The album was recorded as a gift to these young people and attempts to connect the dots from the socially conscious soul

2. "Hard Times," on John Legend and The Roots, *Wake Up!* The song is a cover of Baby Huey and the Babysitters' 1971 song of the same name on *The Baby Huey Story: The Living Legend* (Chicago: Curtom, 1971). Curtis Mayfield wrote the song for Baby Huey and produced the album. After Baby Huey's untimely death in 1971, Mayfield released the song himself as well as track 6 on *There's No Place like America Today* (Chicago: Curtom, 1975).

3. "Shine," on John Legend and The Roots, *Wake Up!*

music of the civil rights era to the new birth of activism today.[4] Rather than simply give in to the lowest common denominator of music stars seeking individual celebrity and enjoying conspicuous consumption, The Roots and Legend attempt to show a collaborative, communal approach to making music, a process less about their own egos and more about the world they fervently desire to live in.[5] Indeed, they go so far as to make the theological claim that in this shared work for good, God lives through us. The songs, the album as a whole, and the musicians behind it offer a bridge into this book, itself a call to "wake up" to the challenges facing the church in responding to the needs of the world God loves.

What Is Fieldwork in Theology?

The church, along with humanity and the earth as a whole, faces deep challenges we are unlikely to meet without just such collaboration, imagination, and passion. My own church, the Evangelical Lutheran Church in America, and churches of North America are emerging from a long history of empire. What some have called the "era of Christendom," begun with Constantine's vision at Milvian Bridge outside Rome in 330 CE, has dramatically ended. Admittedly, in some places, such as in the American South or in my own area of the country, the upper Midwest, the intoxicating aroma of Christendom's opiate haze lingers, blinding people to the sharp contours of the church's new relation to nation and creation. But across the

4. Gene Demby, "The Birth of a New Civil Rights Movement," in POLITICO Magazine, accessed January 22, 2015, http://www.politico.com/magazine/story/2014/12/ferguson-new-civil-rights-movement-113906.html#.VMFHmorF_Wc.

5. Angus Batey, "John Legend and the Roots: Hearts, Minds and Soul," in *The Guardian*, October 19, 2010, http://www.theguardian.com/music/2010/oct/19/john-legend-roots-interview-obama. See also Questlove, *Mo'Meta Blues: The World according to Questlove* (New York: Hachette, 2013).

North Atlantic nations, including Europe, North America, and their far-flung influences, especially Australia and New Zealand, First World Christians face a new reality. In response, there is a new vitality of mission. Christians are asking how they might "wake up" to the Spirit's invitation to get involved in God's love for the world and share in the passion of Jesus Christ in the midst of suffering, healing, reconciling, and doing justice. I will now turn to these themes regarding our social reality today. They provide the crucial context for and urgency of the central argument of this book.

However, before turning to describe this context more fully, I need to pause and state clearly my argument in the book. In doing so, I will briefly sketch the theoretical and theological territory covered in the chapters to follow, offering a view of the forest before we follow the trail through the trees.

Vitality of Christian faith today does not—*and does*—depend on us. Let me explain. Our capacity to live, breathe, and engage in our daily tasks, let alone our ability to find healing and new life in the midst of sin and brokenness, depend fully on the mercy and love of God who comes near to us in the passion of Jesus. Yet as we are met and marked by this Holy One, God's Spirit animates our faithful attempt to be such mercy and love for all who suffer—people as well as the creation. Here the argument of this book comes into play. Turned from sin and joined to God's mission of loving and healing the world, how do we as Christians, the body of Christ, understand the complexity of this beautiful and broken world? My argument is that the task of understanding requires a careful, disciplined craft for inquiry—a craft I call fieldwork in theology—if one seeks both to claim knowledge of divine action and to discern an appropriate human response. The social science of Pierre Bourdieu, in both its origins and influences, offers a way to do disciplined fieldwork in theology leading to clarity of understanding. This may serve the Spirit's call for the church to get involved in what God is doing in the world.

Fieldwork in *Theology*: Williams

As I said above, one of the key challenges to take account of
today is what some call the church's post-Constantinian reality. In the Latin West, we have lived under the long shadow of
Emperor Constantine's conversion to Christian faith and the
subsequent Edict of Milan in February 313, which offered official acceptance of Christianity. The unity of church with the
power of empire for over a thousand years created the circumstance of what I'll call here the church's "establishment" as the
official religion, upheld both politically and culturally. In fact,
Constantine was the one who initiated the long-held practice
of treating Sunday as a sacred day of rest and legislating the
closure of markets on that day as a result. The breakdown of
Constantine's legacy led to a series of disestablishments of the
church in the West, including not only the separation of church
and state but also the rising pluralism of belief—along with
rising numbers of nonbelievers—adding a cultural disestablishment to the political.[6] We are now living, some have argued,
in a secular age.[7]

Responses to a Post-Constantinian Era

Today, two main positions exist with respect to mission in
response to this changing and in some places *already* changed

6. Philip E. Hammond, in *Religion and Personal Autonomy: The Third Disestablishment in America* (Columbia: University of South Carolina Press, 1992),
describes these various moments of the breakup of the Constantinian compromise. He merged religious and political power in the West and institutionalized
it in law, including establishing the first "blue laws," which required businesses to
close on Sunday. Hammond describes the three moments of disestablishment as:
legal separation of church and state (18th century), cultural separation of church
and state (20th century), and personal disconnection from the institution of the
church (especially since the 1960s).

7. Charles Taylor, *A Secular Age* (Cambridge, MA: Belknap, 2007); James
K. A. Smith, *How (Not) to Be Secular: Reading Charles Taylor* (Grand Rapids:
Eerdmans, 2014).

circumstance known as the post-Constantinian era. One might construe the two positions as follows. In the first, the church withdraws *from* the world for the sake of forming a clear Christian identity over against the world. In the second, the church enacts an anarchic "giving away" of itself *in and for* the sake of the world. Obviously these are what Max Weber called "ideal types," which work as analytic positions but don't exist so neatly in lived form.[8] Still, they have lively voices arguing in their favor. Their trajectories directly impact our effort to develop a toolbox for mission, including the craft of fieldwork in theology.

Stanley Hauerwas and William Willimon published the influential book *Resident Aliens* twenty-five years ago as of this writing. They intended the book to provoke a church in transition and change. Instead of simply offering strategic advice as so many texts on church health and growth had, they drew from deep biblical and theological wells to inform their project. They begin in the book by quoting the well-known Christ hymn in Philippians 2. The authors add a brief snippet of Philippians 3 and draw upon the idea of "our commonwealth" being "in heaven" to develop the idea of disciples of Jesus Christ as "resident aliens," those who are in this world but whose true home is elsewhere.[9] This assertion is needed, they say, because the world has changed, and we are now no longer supported by the Constantinian compromise in which Christianity merged with the official powers of society.

Yet the center of the Christ hymn is a claim about the core of God's work in the life, death, and resurrection of the rabbi of Nazareth: humility and self-emptying—or, drawing on a commonly used Greek term, *kenōsis*—in and for the sake of the world. Ironically, the rhetoric and substance of *Resident Aliens* continually turns on an embattled consolidation of identity

8. See Hans Gerth and C. Wright Mills, *From Max Weber: Essays in Sociology* (New York: Oxford University Press, 1946), 59.

9. Stanley Hauerwas and William Willimon, *Resident Aliens: Life in the Christian Colony* (Nashville: Abingdon, 1989), 7, 11.

and action over against the world. For instance, Hauerwas and Willimon write, "In fact, we are not called to help people. We're called to follow Jesus."[10] At a time when many formerly established churches, especially the broad mainstream evangelical and liberal Protestant denominations, find themselves losing cultural establishment, the rhetoric of the book has offered a path for defining a new identity of Christians as an embattled "minority" despite remaining the overwhelming majority in all regions of the United States.[11] Further, the book and its aftermath have sparked a focus on Christian formation, on worship and discipleship within the church, as itself an ethical witness to the world. As they put it, "The church doesn't have a social strategy, the church is a social strategy."[12] Among the many things that could be said about this view, it does not easily lend itself to a humble, grounded, curious approach toward understanding the other. There is no place, no *need* for a place, for the craft of fieldwork in theology.

Twenty years before *Resident Aliens* was published, Anglican theologian Donald MacKinnon gave the Gore Lecture at Westminster Abbey titled "Kenosis and Establishment." This famous London church is the archetype of an establishment church: it has been the site of royal coronations (and often weddings and burials) since William the Conqueror on Christmas Day in 1066.[13] In his lecture, MacKinnon, who was at the time Norris-Hulse Professor of Divinity at Cambridge University, presents a markedly different position from *Resident Aliens*. He favorably quotes "Father R. M. Benson, founder of the Society of St. John the Evangelist, that the conversion of Constantine was the greatest single disaster ever to overtake the Christian

10. Ibid., 121.
11. Robert P. Jones and Melissa C. Stewart, "The Unintended Consequences of Dixieland Postliberalism," *Crosscurrents* (Winter 2006): 506–21.
12. Hauerwas and Willimon, *Resident Aliens*, 43.
13. The abbey has a wonderfully detailed and designed website. See http://www.westminster-abbey.org/our-history.

church."[14] However, after expressing "heartfelt agreement," he goes on to remark that the advent of the post-Constantinian age offers both unparalleled opportunity as well as profound testing to the church. MacKinnon then begins where Hauerwas and Willimon begin: with Philippians 2, with an accounting of the "costliness of the incarnate life to the absolute."[15] Rather than highlighting the invitation to "resident alien" status, however, MacKinnon invites an inhabiting of discipleship shaped according to a radical self-emptying at the heart of the Philippians text. The term for such self-giving, *kenōsis*, functions for MacKinnon as a key idea "for the renewal of the church's understanding of mission."[16]

The rhetoric and substance of his argument do not underwrite a kind of Christian withdrawal by consolidating identity over against the world as in the case of *Resident Aliens*, but rather entail an acceptance of dispossession in and for the world. "To live as a Christian in the world today is necessarily to live an exposed life; it is to be stripped of the kind of security that tradition, whether ecclesiological or institutional, easily bestows."[17] His argument resolutely outlines the losses and difficulties of such a life.

To begin, MacKinnon uses the implications of *kenōsis* to juxtapose contemporary dependence on the church as an established institution versus Jesus's own remarkable dependence on his father. Referring not only to the famous passage from Philippians 2

14. Donald MacKinnon, "Kenosis and Establishment," in *The Stripping of the Altars* (London: Fontana, 1969), 15.

15. Ibid., 17.

16. There is a long and problematic history of this term both in biblical studies and in theology. For the first, my colleague David Frederickson has done very significant work; see "The Kenosis of Christ in the Politics of Paul," *Journal of Lutheran Ethics* (April 2005): http://downloads.elca.org/html/jle/www.elca .org/what-we-believe/social-issues/the-kenosis-of-christ-in-the-politics-6deb5a67 .htm. Theologically, Rowan Williams traces some of the important literature in "Incarnation and the Renewal of Community," in *On Christian Theology* (New York: Blackwell, 2000), 225–38.

17. MacKinnon, "Kenosis and Establishment," 17.

but also to the Fourth Gospel, MacKinnon writes that Jesus depended on an authority "because of and in the context of a supreme humility."[18] That supreme humility is shorthand for the core biblical text on *kenōsis*: "Christ Jesus, who, though he was in the form of God, did not regard equality with God as something to be exploited, but emptied himself, taking the form of a slave, being born in human likeness. And being found in human form, he humbled himself and became obedient to the point of death—even death on a cross" (Phil. 2:6–8).

In this text, MacKinnon finds a chistological "key" to an adequate theology. Attending to the humility and receptivity of Jesus shows us a way to critique false gods of security and autonomy that we set up to bolster our traditions. It is crucial for MacKinnon's Christology to claim that the way of Jesus's self-emptying belongs to God "as he is in himself." When this is true, then he can rightly claim that in Jesus we meet God's "very self and essence." He spells this out by suggesting Jesus's ministry was not merely pointing to God's action, but rather actually embodying it. He writes: Jesus's "invitation to the outcast is not adequately seen as a mere parable of the divine invitation, but rather as its actuality become event."[19] Here it becomes clear that MacKinnon is taking the notion of *kenōsis* and all it represents for Jesus's birth, life, and death on the cross back into God's fundamental act of self-giving that is the incarnation, the word-made-flesh. Such claims have profound implications for a theology of the Trinity, especially debates about the so-called economic and the immanent Trinity.[20] However, our direction turns instead with MacKinnon to the implications for ecclesiology.

In terms of ecclesiology, the relevance of the christological concept of *kenōsis* is arguably difficult to formulate, MacKinnon argues, exactly because our vision of the God-human

18. Ibid.
19. Ibid., 24.
20. A classic text on the relation of economic and immanent trinity is Karl Rahner, *The Trinity* (New York: Continuum, 1970), 21.

relationship is obscured by the sinful reality of the church as human institution. He laments that divine life comes into this world through a "radically distorted image presented in and by the institution supposed to convey its sense to the world."[21] Such a strong claim naturally leads to criticism of the church's institutional experience, including "even rejection of long tracts of that experience as fundamentally invalid."[22] Its Constantinian intertwining with the machinery of war is a case-in-point for such experience. Were the church's status as a state church to finally end, MacKinnon then imagines "a day in which Episcopal lawn sleeves would cease to flutter in the breeze as their wearer bestowed the diocesan benediction upon the latest Polaris submarine. Here we should find sheer gain without any loss at all."[23] He here offers sharp criticism of the malformation of the church but also implicitly raises the question of missional imagination and formation. Thus it is not surprising to see MacKinnon suggest that our first duty is to free our imaginations. The path toward this is, as I said at the start, living into the practice of "exposure" or "stripping," what Rowan Williams calls "the practice of dispossession."[24]

Rowan Williams and the Practice of Dispossession

What, then, might Williams mean by his phrase "the practice of dispossession" in the context of writing about theology of mission, and how might it help us think through our effort to introduce the theological side of fieldwork in theology? In his 1991 Berkeley Divinity School lectures on mission and spirituality, Williams remarked that the word *mission* is not found in the New Testament. An awkward starting point to be sure, but his

21. MacKinnon, "Kenosis and Establishment," 18.
22. Ibid.
23. Ibid., 32.
24. Rowan Williams, *A Ray of Darkness: Sermons and Reflections* (Cambridge, MA: Cowley, 1995), 231.

point in this observation is that in order to talk about mission and the Christian faith, one must first of all "plot" one's path on the map of the New Testament.[25] Williams remarks that while *mission* is not a prominent term in the New Testament, Scripture does speak of "sending": a God who sends Jesus, and Jesus who in the Spirit sends us. In one remarkable verse, Jesus's identity is equated with being sent: in Hebrews 3:1 he is called the *apostolos*, the one who is sent. This sending is for the sake of the world, specifically the poor, the prisoner, the blind, and the oppressed (Luke 4:18). Jesus's "mission," if you will, is not first of all the delivery of a message to believe in but rather a person to whom one responds in action and practice. It is the very reality of Jesus coming to be in relationship with those to whom he was sent. Williams approvingly quotes Hans Urs von Balthasar: "The act of sending grounds the entire earthly existence of Jesus."[26]

This point is central for Williams: "In Jesus person and mission are identical."[27] While humans suffer enmity toward and violence from others, Jesus is the "one for others," such that his very being is an expression of unreserved communion. While his crucifixion was a rejection of this divine action of the offer of communion in and through Jesus, to believe in his resurrection is to say that his radical communion is now reality. His resurrection is the reality that he goes before us and that mission is being sent in his name as part of that reconciling work of new communion. Here Williams shows that the articulation of Jesus's identity and mission leads us into the presence of the trinitarian life. "If we want to speak adequately of mission, we have to speak of the Trinity, of God's life as communion."[28] Our experience of Jesus and of his life of self-giving for the

25. Ibid., 221.
26. Hans Urs von Balthasar, *Theodramatik II: Die Personen des Spiels, Teil 2: Die Personen in Christus* (Einsiedeln: Johannes, 1978), 140.
27. Williams, *Ray of Darkness*, 222.
28. Ibid., 225.

sake of new community leads us to an understanding of God as three-in-one, communion in essence. But God also returns to the world through this very same trinitarian life, outpouring as wisdom and word in the power of the Spirit. Thus, as Williams puts it, "Mission is a matter of *dispossession*. Jesus is God's giving-away, a holding nothing back: all the Father has is given to Jesus (John 16:10)."[29]

As if all too aware of the abstract nature of all this reflection, Williams sets forth several implications that will figure into our taking up dispossession as a crucial theological feature of the craft of fieldwork in theology. First, he says in no uncertain terms that "there is no gap between the gospel and life together."[30] Each congregation may fall short, be subject to division and fear, yet by virtue of its very life the church presses against the sources of division and fear to engage in radical communion with others. Rather than finding a sort of self-satisfaction and false sense of completeness in itself (Hauerwas and Willimon's "life in the Christian colony"), a humble posture is willing to engage rigorous self-critique. Acknowledging the incompleteness then drives the church's openness to the other and in fact to the whole world. In this act of reaching out, of giving itself away to others, the church finds its very identity.

Second, in its call to communion, the church has a very specific responsibility to "the one," recalling Jesus's famous "lost" parables in Luke 15. Rather than seeking a disembodied home elsewhere (what Hauerwas and Willimon claim as our goal— "a colony of heaven"), the logic of *kenōsis* is God's sending of an incarnate one who takes on flesh and dwells among us (John 1:14), especially to those who are "disenfranchised by whatever context they live in."[31] While of course it rejoices in those who are already well, the church, like its Lord, is sent out in particular for the sake of the sick, the lost, the hungry, the

29. Ibid.
30. Ibid.
31. Ibid., 227.

hurting, and the hopeless. The Johannine "dwelt among us" importantly extends to "any and every creature ('Preach the gospel to every creature')."[32]

Third, given that the church is, as Williams says, "a flawed and often profoundly unimpressive historical reality," mission involves repentance.[33] Rather than positing an ideal ecclesiology regarding communion, we can rest in "the indestructibility of God's commitment" so that an actual account of the challenges of communion are faced. The practice of dispossession applies here also. Jesus's activity as the "sent one" gives us a new way of being in community. We as church are caught up in this giving away of ourselves for the sake of others, specifically "asking how *their* way of receiving the gospel enlarges what we can see and know of the gospel."[34] In fact, the incarnation as part of God's life lived for us, for communion with creatures and creation, makes sense for our lives only in relation to the concrete, daily realities of the actual church in the real world in all its beauty and brokenness.[35]

Finally, Williams helps to guard against letting our language about incarnation and Trinity "become a system for our intellectual or institutional possession: it is only plausible or authoritative, only makes sense, within the practice of dispossession, an authentically self-forgetting practice that allows and nourishes the otherness of others."[36] Williams compels us to recognize that fieldwork in theology is not as simple as the instructions one receives for using a new phone or computer. Rather, by using the practice of dispossession to frame our understanding of the "theology" side of fieldwork in theology, we are invited into life with Jesus, sent by the Spirit, which

32. Ibid., 229. Here Williams is quoting Mark 16:15 (KJV).
33. Ibid.
34. Ibid., 230.
35. See Nicholas M. Healy's reflections on ideal and concrete ecclesiology in *Church, World and the Christian Life: Practical-Prophetic Ecclesiology* (New York: Cambridge University Press, 2000), 39.
36. Williams, *Ray of Darkness*, 231.

opens opportunities for communion we are not in control of. Mission as dispossession, being caught up in Jesus's own life in the Spirit, is a *gift* and therefore must be given freely to see what shape communion takes.

Fieldwork in Theology: Bourdieu

While this whole book functions as an introduction to Bourdieu, a brief overview will help make sense of his place in the field and also set up the particular sort of theological work I develop in relationship to his social science. While it might be typical to start with his date of birth and key facts of his biography, Bourdieu's own sketch of his life takes a different tack. We are, Bourdieu claims, shaped by a particular "field," by which he means the concrete social context of our life. Further, he would argue, what is shaped in us via the formative practice within a field is a "*habitus*," or mode of being in the world, by which we practically navigate day-to-day life. I'll say much more about the emergence of these concepts in Bourdieu's empirical work, and how they might be useful tools for our own fieldwork in theology, in chapter 4. If this all feels confusing, I invite you to set aside your doubts and keep reading—the complexity will feel intense but hopefully patience will give way to growing clarity and understanding, opening the possibility of renewed engagement in the craft of fieldwork.

One way of facing complexity is by drawing on a tradition of theology claiming that the Christian life is lived as "simultaneously saint and sinner" (*simul justus et peccator*).[37] This perspective might be called paradoxical: Really, you might say, saint *and* sinner simultaneously? This might explain why I am so drawn to Bourdieu, who is quite a paradoxical thinker. (The term, *paradox*, from the ancient Greek *paradoxos*, meaning

37. Robert Kolb and Charles Arand, *The Genius of Luther's Theology* (Grand Rapids: Baker Academic, 2008), 49.

"unexpected," here carries the meaning of "holding two seemingly contradictory ideas as both true.") Again and again Bourdieu marshals seeming opposites in very fruitful ways as he navigates the academic worlds of philosophy and social science. I'll use this notion of paradox as a starting point for an outline of the professional academic field out of which his "reflexive sociology" developed before turning to discuss two main misunderstandings of Bourdieu.[38]

Bourdieu's Formation in the Academic Field

The best introduction to Bourdieu's method for social research and its philosophical and practical commitments is through his formation in the academic field and in relationship to major scholarly influences, including mentors and colleagues. The first and perhaps most-often cited influences I discuss, Jean-Paul Sartre and Claude Lévi-Strauss, were the dominant intellectual forces of his early years in the academic world of post–World War II France. The second major shaping force comes from the founders of his discipline of sociology, Émile Durkheim, Max Weber, and Karl Marx. Drawing from each, Bourdieu marshaled resources to critique contemporary forms of social science both in Europe and in the United States. The third major shaping force is the result of his exposure to influential teachers, from Gaston Bachelard to Maurice Merleau-Ponty.

BOURDIEU BETWEEN SARTRE AND LÉVI-STRAUSS

I first encountered Bourdieu by reading his mid-1970s work *Outline of a Theory of Practice*, a book written largely as a critique of objectivism and the way it was present in an academic school of thought called structuralism. Structuralism

---

38. Pierre Bourdieu, *Esquisse pour une auto-analyse* (Paris: Éditions Raisons d'Agir, 2004); translated by Richard Nice as *Sketch for a Self-Analysis* (Chicago: University of Chicago Press, 2008). Bourdieu writes in the epigraph, "This is not an autobiography."

argued that human culture must be understood in terms of an overarching logic or structure. In Bourdieu's formative years, the French anthropologist Claude Lévi-Strauss was the leading figure of the structuralism school. Bourdieu himself worked from a version of structuralism in the late 1950s and early 1960s but grew critical of its "tendency to *intellectualism* implied in observing language from the standpoint of the listening subject rather than that of the speaking subject."[39] While continuing to hold a key place for the importance of objective structures of society in shaping our everyday lives, Bourdieu clearly names the problem with the uncritical stance of the scholar's point of view typical in structuralism. He writes,

> So long as he remains unaware of the limits inherent in his point of view on the object, the anthropologist is condemned to adopt unwittingly for his own use the representation of action which is forced on agents or groups when they lack practical mastery of a highly valued competence and have to provide themselves with an explicit and at least semi-formalized substitute for it in the form of a *repertoire of rules*.[40]

The attraction and danger of such an approach becomes clear with the example of a map.[41] A map benefits the outside observer who needs to find her way around an unfamiliar landscape. Without the practical ability of the local person who knows particular paths, the outsider uses a model of all possible routes. Structuralism imagines the map and regulated patterns of traveling through the territory on the map as an accurate depiction of what is unconsciously going on in the minds of individuals traveling from place to place. Their actions are

39. Pierre Bourdieu, *Outline of a Theory of Practice*, trans. Richard Nice (Cambridge: Cambridge University Press, 1977), 1.

40. Ibid., 2, emphasis original. First, it is important to remember that Bourdieu positioned his early work more in relation to anthropology and later to sociology, but second, in Europe the distinctions between discrete areas in social science are not as demarcated as in the United States.

41. Ibid.

determined by the structure of the map. Yet knowing all the possible routes, or even the patterns of routes, typically taken by the locals determines only the formal logic of the rule of traveling from one location to another. It does not account for the practical use of these routes by actual people in their everyday lives, which is decided by the unconscious practical logic Bourdieu terms "invention within limits."[42]

By his critique of the objective side of the debate about human action, he might seem to be supportive of the other side, a more subjective articulation of radical human freedom to act in each moment as an exercise of pure will. In Bourdieu's formative years, the French philosopher Jean-Paul Sartre, a leading figure in existential phenomenology, publically argued for this point of view. Bourdieu, highlighting his desire to find a middle ground between objectivism and subjectivism, writes,

> But the rejection of the mechanistic theories in no way implies that, in accordance with another obligatory option, we should bestow on some creative free will the free and willful power to constitute, on the instant, the meaning of the situation by projecting the ends aiming at its transformation, and that we should reduce the objective intentions and constituted significations of actions and works to the conscious and deliberate intentions of their authors.[43]

Bourdieu argues it is a false dilemma to say that one's choices are either determined by a dominant social structure or totally free relative to one's conscious intention.

He also refuses the dichotomy of personal spontaneity versus social constraint. Instead, he takes these as paradoxically interconnected; they exist in dialectical relationship within actual lived practice. Exactly because of his careful fieldwork and the concepts—practice, *habitus*, and field—that account for the

42. Ibid., 96.
43. Ibid., 73.

practical logic of everyday strategies of living, Bourdieu's approach leads to deeper understanding of the real relationships shaping and being shaped by our lives.[44]

BOURDIEU BETWEEN MARX, WEBER, AND DURKHEIM

Bourdieu's commitment to fieldwork, the careful study of social relations as a means to understanding culture and society, is rooted in his reading of the great founders of social science, Karl Marx, Max Weber, and Émile Durkheim. Of course, their particular studies, concepts, and theories had distinct influences on Bourdieu's own research projects. At a more basic level, however, Bourdieu sought to "return to the sources" to reorient the whole discipline of sociology away from the twin dangers of the theoretical sociologist, an approach without any grounding in social research, and the positivist sociologist, who commits the opposite error.[45] His goal was to "engage in theoretically grounded empirical research."[46] His clarity on the need for this turn in sociology emerged during his early years as a professor in Paris.

While serving his required military deployment in Algeria, Bourdieu became acquainted with Raymond Aron, a professor of sociology at the Sorbonne in Paris, who invited him to be his assistant. With his sponsorship, Bourdieu published his first book, which was based on fieldwork he carried out while stationed in Algeria, and he was subsequently elected to the faculty at *École de hautes études en sciences sociales*.[47] During these years, he simultaneously continued to carry out research

44. Pierre Bourdieu and Loïc Wacquant, *An Invitation to Reflexive Sociology* (Chicago: University of Chicago Press, 1992), 22–23. I'll have much more to say on the development and use of his fieldwork practice and the concepts developed from it in chap. 4 below.

45. Pierre Bourdieu, Jean-Claude Chamboredon, and Jean-Claude Passeron, *The Craft of Sociology: Epistemological Preliminaries* (Berlin: de Gruyter, 1991), 16n5, 248.

46. Bourdieu, *Sketch for a Self-Analysis*, 73.

47. Pierre Bourdieu, *The Algerians* (Boston: Beacon, 1962).

and publish while also offering seminars in sociology. Out of one seminar on epistemology, the theory of knowledge, co-taught by Bourdieu and his colleague Jean-Claude Passeron, Bourdieu recognized he was "putting into practice a methodology that had not been made explicit."[48] *The Craft of Sociology* was the result.

At the heart of the book, Bourdieu and his coauthors draw on the founders of their discipline—Marx, Weber, and Durkheim—for a theory of knowledge, especially regarding what they label the "illusion of transparency" to which members of society tend to be inclined. They write,

> Durkheim, who insists that the sociologist must enter the social world as one enters an unknown world, gives Marx the credit for having broken the illusion of transparency: "We think it a fertile idea that social life must be explained, not by the conception of it created by those who participate in it, but by profound causes which escape awareness."[49]

In sum, the meaning of social life is not simply reducible to individual ideas and actions and self-consciousness of them. Rather, the craft of sociology begins by a *break* with common sense, pursuing research on the basis of the claim that the full meaning of social life is more than what is consciously available to a person or group.[50]

BOURDIEU BETWEEN BACHELARD AND MERLEAU-PONTY

Michel Foucault, a contemporary of Bourdieu who shared many influences and common commitments, divides the academic world within which they both came of age. On the one side, he places "philosophers of experience, of sense and of subject" and on the other, "a philosophy of knowledge, of

---

48. Bourdieu, Chamboredon, and Passeron, *Craft of Sociology*, 247.
49. Ibid., 15.
50. In one paragraph, Bourdieu and his coauthors cite Durkheim, Marx, and Weber on this point (*Craft of Sociology*, 15).

rationality and of concept."[51] With the first, Foucault places Jean-Paul Sartre and Maurice Merleau-Ponty. With the second, he names Gaston Bachelard and Georges Canguilhem. Here again, Bourdieu takes seeming opposites and finds a paradoxical path between both. Yet in this third instance of scholarly formation, we come up against academic names that, however important for Bourdieu's own development, have not risen to the fore as key interlocutors in analyses of his work in the English-speaking world. Bachelard and Merleau-Ponty each receive a full chapter later in the book, itself a statement of my own conviction about their centrality. In advance of those chapters, a broad framing of the issues and views shaping our approach to Bourdieu's own work might be helpful as we navigate our way forward.

Gaston Bachelard was a historian and philosopher of science who taught at the Sorbonne in Paris during the 1950s. Critical of prior generations of thinkers—most famously René Descartes—who began their scientific work on the basis of a priori claims for the foundations of reason and knowledge, Bachelard argues for specific histories of reason. His famous concepts—especially the idea of the "epistemological break"— are immediately visible in Bourdieu's own work. The first use of an epistemological break is in the break with common sense, a move outlined above in relation to the classical founders of sociology. Science must, Bachelard argued, begin by breaking with what Nietzsche called the "dogma of immaculate perception," a playful way of naming the temptation to take one's ordinary sense perception as trustworthy.[52] Second, however, science proceeds by overcoming "epistemological obstacles" and so makes progress through discontinuity and breaks with past understanding. Bachelard's successor, Georges Canguilhem, an

51. Michel Foucault, introduction to Georges Canguilhem, *The Normal and the Pathological* (New York: Zone, 1991).

52. Friedrich Nietzsche, *Thus Spake Zarathustra* (New York: Penguin, 1961), 100.

important teacher and mentor for Bourdieu, termed this the "priority of error" in science.

Another important implication of Bachelard's approach to the history of science lies in his claim that social facts are constructed—knowledge is no longer viewed as a mere reflection of reality but as a result of scientific invention through the craft of field research. Here Bourdieu quotes Bachelard: "The orientation of the epistemological 'vector' seems clear. It surely points from the rational to the real and not, as all philosophers from Aristotle to Bacon professed, from the real to the general."[53] As a result, Bourdieu argues, "you don't move to the real without a hypothesis, without instruments of construction. And when you think you are without presuppositions, you still construct without knowing it and, in that case, almost always inadequately." It is, he argues, a particular imperative in sociology to break from simply converting "social problems" into "sociological problems."[54]

A second break, beyond breaking from commonsense perceptions, is to make the position of the social scientist an object of critique. Bourdieu writes,

> It is not sufficient for anthropology to break with native experience and the native representation of that experience: it has to make a second break and question the presuppositions inherent in the position of the outside observer, who in his preoccupation with interpreting practices, is included to introduce into the object the principles of his relation to the object.[55]

The focus here is not simply the individual observer but the social world inhabited by the observer and the analytic tools marshaled for the work as part of the collective enterprise of science. Taking the researcher and the research practice itself

53. Gaston Bachelard, *The New Scientific Spirit* (Boston: Beacon, 1984), 4.
54. Bourdieu, Chamboredon, and Passeron, *Craft of Sociology*, 248–49.
55. Bourdieu, *Outline of a Theory*, 2.

as an object of the research, however, does not undercut the process. To the contrary, such reflexivity strengthens both the practice of research and its findings.[56] It is exactly this approach that allows Bourdieu to critique Lévi-Strauss's structuralism and its privileging of the scholar's view (the "map") over the ordinary person's practical mastery (of particular paths).

Bourdieu once stated in an interview that "sociology is a very difficult science. You're always steering between two opposite dangers; you can easily jump from the frying-pan into the fire. That's why I've spent my life demolishing dualisms."[57] Fully incorporating the second break, just discussed above, forced Bourdieu out of his position as "a blissful structuralist."[58] Seeking a paradoxical pathway between structuralism and existentialism, between Lévi-Strauss and Sartre, led Bourdieu to draw deeply from Maurice Merleau-Ponty, especially in developing his concept of the *habitus*. He comments on needing to account for practices of gender division in an Algerian peasant household, for example, and finding them at once unconscious and systematic. He looked to Merleau-Ponty's work on incorporated dispositions and what he called "the body schema" as a means to do this.[59]

Merleau-Ponty was professor of philosophy at the Sorbonne and then the Collège de France. He studied phenomenology, especially the work of Edmund Husserl and Martin Heidegger. For Bourdieu, Merleau-Ponty's most important contribution was incorporation of the body into Heidegger's phenomenology of "being-in-the-world."[60] In overcoming the subject-object split dominant in the West since Descartes, Heidegger posited a preconscious notion captured by this "compound expression" that

56. Bourdieu and Wacquant, *Invitation to Reflexive Sociology*, 36.
57. Bourdieu, Chamboredon, and Passeron, *Craft of Sociology*, 251.
58. Bourdieu, *The Logic of Practice* (Stanford: Stanford University Press, 1992), 9.
59. Ibid., 10.
60. Martin Heidegger, *Being and Time* (New York: HarperCollins, 1962), 78.

stands for a "unitary phenomenon."[61] That unitary phenomenon could be put this way: one's world is that particular reality into which one is born and where one learns what it means to live a meaningful life. In this sense, it is better to say one *has* a world than to say there *is* a world. The first shows the relational connection, as if to be at all is to have a world in which to be, whereas the second implies a chasm between one and the world.

The crucial development of describing the role of the body and its perception of the world used the body's very corporality as a means to overcome the dualism of object and subject. Merleau-Ponty puts it this way: "I *have* the world as an unfinished individual through my body as a power for this world . . . because my body is a movement toward the world and because the world is my body's support."[62] Bourdieu puts it thus: "We are disposed because we are exposed."[63] Our bodies learn the world into which we are born, and we have the world within us. Bourdieu, drawing explicitly on Merleau-Ponty, describes *habitus* as a particular but constant way of entering into relationship with the world the body inhabits. We "inhabit the world like a garment [*un habit*] or a familiar habitat."[64] The body works, as it were, as social memory and knows how to be and act as if by "second nature."

A brief example from my own research practice might help in both clarifying and integrating some of these matters for our orientation to Bourdieu's academic formation in mid-twentieth-century France and North Africa. In the late 1990s, I did my first fieldwork in theology as part of a project aimed at understanding the culture, community, and political life of three old downtown congregations in Atlanta, Georgia. I had just spent

61. Ibid.
62. Maurice Merleau-Ponty, *Phenomenology of Perception* (New York: Routledge, 1962), 366.
63. Pierre Bourdieu, *Pascalian Meditations* (Stanford: Stanford University Press, 2000), 140.
64. Ibid., 142.

approximately six months researching an African Methodist Episcopal congregation deeply impacted by the neo-Pentecostal movement.[65] Afterward, I was having a difficult time recalibrating my skills of perception at the downtown Presbyterian congregation. After one Sunday, I commented in my field notes,

> I noted more today than before that the congregation almost never responds to what is said or proclaimed from the front except with formal sung responses, such as the sung response to the declaration of pardon. And when people pray, they literally don't do much more than (at the most) fold or overlay their hands and slightly bow their heads. Many keep looking about, keeping the exact posture they had before, like the man in front of me who had his right leg over his left, torso turned slightly to the left, shoulders tilted that way. He was picking his fingernails, which he continued to do through the prayer.

First, then, in this situation, I needed to break with common-sense experience. Through my observation, what I could see was a limited and ultimately not very helpful set of factors with which to try to understand the congregation. Second, I needed to construct my view of the congregation systematically, using research tools to gain deeper access to their circumstances. As I had at other congregations, I began to interview people to begin to see with their eyes and worship with them to begin to feel as they feel in their bodies, thus gaining fuller insight into the particularities of their life together.

One longtime member gave me this description of his worship experience:

> You know, during and after worship, but at points *during* worship, I mean I'm moved, I'm emotionally moved, and I was

65. For more on the neo-Pentecostal movement among the AME Church, see Lawrence H. Mamiya, "A Social History of the Bethel African Methodist Episcopal Church in Baltimore," in James P. Wind and James W. Lewis, *American Congregations* (Chicago: University of Chicago Press, 1994), 1:222.

telling someone about this one time, there were people sitting around and I said, you know, I mean I'm a bit of a marshmallow anyway, but I said I was literally moved to tears, and they said, "Oh, God, yea" and I started to realize that as I looked around the congregation, that's when I realized that you got a bunch of people blubbering. How un-Presbyterian can you get? You know, we're not going to get into any more ecstatic modes of worship, I'll tell you that, but for a Presbyterian to shed a tear in worship, holy cow! I can't keep from crying in the service.

Though the congregation was not prone to the sort of visible spiritual ecstasy prominent in neo-Pentecostal style, I nonetheless began to see and feel a distinct sort of passionate and intense worship, whether it was singing, listening, or responding to various call-and-response portions of the service. The interviews informed my observations, and I now noted a much more fine-grained level of bodily movement—eye contact, gestures, facial expressions—that signaled a beginning in understanding members' subtle but powerful modes of embodied engagement.[66]

Main Misunderstandings of Bourdieu

The first main misunderstanding commonly associated with Bourdieu is that he is primarily concerned with theory. As he notes, misreading him as a grand theorist says more about the social context of the reader than it does about his own self-understanding and commitments. Mark Lewis Taylor, the Maxwell M. Upson Professor of Theology and Culture at Princeton Seminary, for example, uses Bourdieu's concept of *habitus* in developing a "dispositional theory of practices."[67] He does not do research

66. This research was published as Christian Scharen, *Public Work and Public Worship* (Collegeville, MO: Liturgical Press, 2004).
67. Mark Lewis Taylor, *The Theological and the Political: On the Weight of the World* (Minneapolis: Fortress, 2011), esp. chap. 2.

and is not particularly interested in Bourdieu's, either. Taylor, as do some sociologists and also many theologians, works with what Bourdieu calls "theoreticist theory." By this term Bourdieu means discourse originating by dissection or by amalgamation of other theories.[68] In a rare moment when he directly addresses misunderstandings of his work, Bourdieu writes,

> The clearest misunderstanding stems from the fact that the lector's reading is an end in itself, and that it is interested in texts, and in the theories, methods or concepts that they convey, not in order to do something with them, to bring them, as useful, perfectible instruments, into a practical use, but so as to gloss them, by relating them to other texts (under cover, on occasion, of epistemology or methodology). This reading thus sweeps away what is essential, that is to say, not only the problems that the concepts aimed to name and resolve—understanding a ritual, explaining the variations in behavior in relation to credit, saving or fertility, accounting for differential rates of educational success or museum-going, etc.—but also the space of theoretical and methodological possibles which led those problems to be posed, at that moment, and in those terms.[69]

For Bourdieu, theory emerges from problems that arise in trying to understand a particular field or social context within a particular research project. Theory or theoretical concepts are like tools one develops for practical use in research practice. The term "possibles," drawn from Gaston Bachelard, suggests a particular way Bourdieu's research procedure operates—that the concepts and research method must fit and follow from the character of what one seeks to understand. Therefore, for Bourdieu, the aim is the "fusion of theoretical construction and practical research."[70] Every act of research is simultaneously empirical and theoretical.

68. Bourdieu and Wacquant, *Invitation to Reflexive Sociology*, 161.
69. Bourdieu, *Pascalian Meditations*, 62.
70. Bourdieu and Wacquant, *Invitation to Reflexive Sociology*, 35.

The second main misunderstanding commonly associated with Bourdieu is viewing him as a determinist, especially regarding social inequality. This misunderstanding typically shows up in claims that Bourdieu's work highlights the forces of domination without accounting for possibilities of liberation from domination. Here, British sociologist Richard Jenkins is a case in point. He mistakes Bourdieu's careful empirical attention to the structure and reproduction of social inequality for a normative claim about the inevitability of such forces to rule out social change.[71]

It is true that social inequality and domination was a major theme in Bourdieu's work—from his first fieldwork among Algerian peasants during the 1950s Algerian War of Independence (his one-year military service was there, and he stayed on, lecturing and doing ethnographic research) to his late-career writings on television, capitalism, and globalization.[72] His studies of the social reproduction of class difference as well as the durability of class distinction and difference point to the power and presence of domination.[73] In fact, he says, "If it is fitting to recall that the dominated always contribute to their own domination, it is necessary at once to be reminded that the dispositions that incline them to this complicity are also the effect, embodied, of domination."[74]

Bourdieu refuses the dichotomy between scientific work and an agenda for social transformation. His hope, in fact, is that

71. His classic article is Richard Jenkins, "Pierre Bourdieu and the Reproduction of Determinism in Sociology," *Sociology* 16, no. 2 (May 1982): 270–81. See also Richard Jenkins, *Pierre Bourdieu* (Key Sociologists), rev. ed. (New York: Routledge, 2002), 82–83.

72. Bourdieu, *Algerians*; Pierre Bourdieu, *On Television* (New York: New Press, 1999).

73. Pierre Bourdieu and Jean-Claude Passeron, *Reproduction in Education, Society and Culture* (London: Sage, 1990); Pierre Bourdieu, *Distinction: A Social Critique of the Judgment of Taste* (Cambridge, MA: Harvard University Press, 1984).

74. Pierre Bourdieu, *The State Nobility: Elite Schools in the Field of Power* (Stanford, CA: Stanford University Press, 1998), 12.

more careful social science will be a more powerful social critique in service of social action for transformation of oppressive social policies. Because of his analysis of the embodiment of domination, it is all the more important to engage in the work of analyzing the characteristics of the social forces and embodied practices particular groups—women, minorities, poor workers—inhabit. Therefore, every act of research is simultaneously scholarship and a social commitment to make a better world.[75]

Outline of the Rest of the Book

These three evocations of the academic field formative for Bourdieu's social science, combined with the discussion of two main misunderstandings, now offer a launch into our shared unpacking of the outline of the rest of the book. With chapter 2, I focus on the rigorous self-reflection in Gaston Bachelard's philosophy of science, connecting it to Rowan Williams's first point about the church's brokenness and humility as it faces the world. Then chapter 3 engages the embodied perception found in Maurice Merleau-Ponty's phenomenology as an entryway into a grounded, fleshly, incarnational approach to being-in-the-world, especially those most on the margins. Chapter 4 delves into Bourdieu's construal of a practical logic that helps us avoid the trap of idealist pictures of the church and instead seeks to understand its concrete reality in communion with the world God loves. Chapter 5 picks up Loïc Wacquant's development of Bourdieu's trajectory, especially his apprenticeship-to-the-other as a theoretically informed practice of field research very conducive to the idea of sacramental "self-giving" to the other, a substantial implication of the logic of incarnation itself.

Along the way, I will tell stories from my own as well as other social scientists' research projects. I came to this theological

75. Pierre Bourdieu, *Political Interventions: Social Science and Political Action* (New York: Verso, 2008), 380–81.

framework by listening carefully to particular congregations and paying attention to their imagination and practice of dispossession as part of an effort of churches to wake up and get involved with what God is up to in the world. The theological reflections of fieldwork in theology are certainly likely to articulate aspects of these congregations' work that they do not articulate themselves. It is an effort to show how the craft of fieldwork in theology offers a disciplined approach to understanding this complex "secular age" and its wide variety of spiritual communities living faith in their own ways.

One thing is clear: leaders of churches of any sort in North America can't take being church for granted. Once people stop just assuming citizenship in a nation equals church membership as part of a normal life trajectory, and once mission becomes the new reality not just in far-off lands but right here in one's local neighborhood, then something like the craft of fieldwork in theology is required. It is, as John Legend and The Roots sing, a vibrant call to "Wake Up" and see how God is at work making a new land. That new land is not some other place. It is a new creation. "See," the prophet Isaiah declared, "I am about to do a new thing; now it springs forth, do you not perceive it?" (Isa. 43:19). In order to engage ministry with vitality, perceive the new things God is doing, and "participate in God," leaders have to get out and learn what's going on and how to relate to the people and context where they are. Fieldwork in theology is that simple—and that complicated![76]

76. Paul S. Fiddes, *Participating in God: A Pastoral Doctrine of the Trinity* (Louisville: Westminster John Knox, 2000).

2

Rigorous Self-Reflection

Bachelard, Science, and Sin

> Gaston Bachelard's philosophy of science is not well known, but his work profoundly influenced Pierre Bourdieu as well as fellow French luminaries Michel Foucault and Jacques Derrida and the American historian of science Thomas Kuhn. All benefited from Bachelard's notion of "epistemological breaks," a key focus for this chapter.

A Prelude from U2: "Bad"

"I'm wide awake, I'm not sleeping," Bono howls, as if seeking to convince the listener simply by force of volume.[1] The line, from the Irish rock band U2's well-known anthem "Bad," seems an odd one to shout out. *Good for you*, the listener might think. *We all have to get up and get on with the day.* However, the song is not clear at face value—it never "says" exactly what it

---

1. "Bad," on U2, *The Unforgettable Fire* (London: Island Records, 1984).

is about but rather evokes it, constructs it, by the technique of sympathetic narrative. To "get" the song requires taking an imaginative leap, at least for most of us.

Bono, lead singer and songwriter for U2, wrote this song in response to rampant heroin addiction in Dublin in the late 1970s and early 1980s. It starts very quietly, with a softly chiming guitar played by The Edge, U2's guitarist. A slight tap of a tambourine adds to the shimmering feel, as if a surreal experience is opening up to the listener. Yet as Bono softly sings the end of the first verse, a persistent, propulsive beat shared between drum and bass guitar pull the listener into the song. The feeling is intended.

To write the song, Bono avoided external, and especially judgmental, frames for interpreting the experience. Rather, his sympathetic narrative embodies two voices: one, a friend desperately desiring to help an addict break free, and the other, the addict, desperately caught in the undertow of the drug. In the book *U2 by U2*, Bono describes young people he and the band knew:

> A lot of sweet teenage kids . . . were offered this cheap high, something beyond their imagination. So, they'd smoke it once a month, then once a week, and they became slaves. They gave up everything they held sacred to this drug. I tried to describe that with the song, Bad, what it was to feel that rush, to feel that elation, and then go on to the nod, the awful sleep that comes with that drug, and then scream: I'm wide awake, I'm wide awake, I'm not sleeping![2]

This last bit of the song follows a litany of feelings evoked by sinking into the heroin-induced daze, including "desperation," "condemnation," "revelation," "temptation," "isolation," "desolation." Desolation appears last as a depiction of the end of the rush experienced by addicts. It fits the haze that

2. U2 and Neil McCormick, *U2 by U2* (New York: IT Books, 2009), 191.

overcomes the user, the "awful sleep" Bono describes. But he does not leave the addict there, in part, of course, because he wrote the song about friends. The cry at the end, "Oh, no / I'm wide awake / I'm not sleeping," is an assertion of the dignity of the human person against the slavery of addiction.

The song really finds its voice, its power, as a live song; its presence in U2's live set list is unrivaled despite competition from their many other hits over the years. It has often been an emotional closer for their live shows, in part because of its visceral musical crescendo, but also because of its depiction of the realities—troubling and hopeful—facing the world around us. Bono says, "'Bad' for me is a song that I use to wake myself up, wake myself up to see the world around me, and what is going on in the world around me."[3]

The song is not necessarily the story one might predict based on the subject matter, however. Given the lives thrown away in addiction, one could expect stories responding in disgust, or with judgment, or a diagnosis of social ills; all would create an object held at arm's length. Instead, through a technique I call sympathetic narrative, Bono seeks to enter into and feel the experience of the other, constructing his story via poetry and song. In this case the story is of a heroin addict, and though it is not Bono's personal experience, it is important for him to tell it truthfully. "If you're true, if you describe what's in your life, or in the room, or what you pick up—because a lot of our songs, I feel like they are overheard conversations. Sometimes they're not my stories, but I feel them very deeply. But to be true is really important, and that seems to get you truth. God is interested in truth, and only in truth."[4]

3. *World in Action: U2, Anthem for the Eighties,* directed by Paul Greengrass, July 27, 1987, based on a 1987 U2 concert in their hometown of Dublin.
4. "Bono: A Conversation: A *New York Times* Event at the Graduate Center of the City University of New York," March 16, 2003, transcribed from audio available at www.nytimes.com/ref/arts/music/20030417talks-bono.html.

Truth, Jesus said, will set us free. It is in a way a liberation
theology in song to attempt such a careful, honest, and hopeful
depiction of being caught in the throes of drug addiction. Such
careful and sympathetic storytelling will not necessarily change
the world by itself, yet it can indeed be part of the equation of
change, shaping an imagination open to being awake, to being
fully human, to being the creature God intended.

From U2 to Bachelard

The interest in truth, and the use of techniques for its construction, presents an opening to our discussion of Gaston Bachelard.
While it is obviously a long way from "Bad" to Bachelard, the
connection works. One cannot, both would say, take things as
they appear on the surface; rather, through careful construction
one can come to a deeper, truer understanding of reality.[5] I briefly
introduced Bachelard in the previous chapter, but it might be
important to recall the context of his early career. When he began
his professorship in the late 1920s, major scientific revisions
were unfolding, including Einstein's general theory of relativ-
ity and Heisenberg's uncertainty principle, a key to quantum
mechanics. These dramatic upheavals in science led Bachelard
to abandon the Enlightenment dream of reason and a singular
path of scientific achievement. Yet he did not fully discard what
came before, choosing instead to show how discontinuity always
builds on the past even as it finds (sometimes radically) new
frameworks of understanding reality. I'll focus my exposition of
his thinking broadly on his non-Cartesian epistemology and the
three key components of this approach to scientific knowledge:
obstacles, breaks, and couples. While this surely sounds peculiar
now, we'll find that it is practical and sensible as well as useful.

5. In this light, it is not surprising to find that in addition to his books on the
philosophy of science, Bachelard also wrote about poetry. See, for example, *The
Poetics of Space* (Boston: Beacon, 1969).

Non-Cartesian Epistemology

René Descartes's influence on generations of scientists was enormous, especially in relationship to two areas: epistemology and scientific method. Characteristic of his approach, Bachelard both rejects and builds on Descartes. First, he rejects the idea that our knowledge of the world is founded on what is often called "reductive foundationalism."[6] Descartes, in his famous *Discourse on Method*, leads the reader along with him as he doubts everything except the fact that he doubts, a procedure that leads him to declare, "I think, therefore I am."[7] Doubting all sense perception, he retreats to the mind's idea of a thing as the true feature of the real, so the "substance" of his person is his mind, with a body as a particular and changing (and thus untrustworthy) extension of the mind (substance). Matter, or substance, and its extension, are a medieval metaphysical framework. To help make more sense of the concepts, let me offer an example, one Bachelard uses to show his "non-Cartesian epistemology."

In his *Meditations on First Philosophy*, Descartes uses the example of some wax in his hand to further explain his ideas. The wax in his hand, he remarks, has a solid feel—hard, cold, with a faint scent of the honey and flowers the bees collected as they produced it. The feel, look, smell, and so on, tell us it is a piece of wax. But when set by the fire, the wax melts into clear liquid and in the process loses every one of the aspects by which our senses told us it was a piece of wax. Because of the unreliability of the senses to tell us what this thing, wax, is in its essence, Descartes therefore concludes the true thing is only perceived "by the mind alone."[8]

6. See Mary Tiles, *Bachelard: Science and Objectivity* (Cambridge: Cambridge University Press, 1984), 39.

7. René Descartes, *Discourse on Method*, in *The Philosophical Writings of Descartes*, vol. 1, trans. John Cottingham, Robert Stoothoff, and Dugald Murdoch (Cambridge: Cambridge University Press, 1985), 127.

8. René Descartes, *Meditations on First Philosophy*, in *The Philosophical Writings of Descartes*, vol. 2, trans. John Cottingham, Robert Stoothoff, and Dugald Murdoch (Cambridge: Cambridge University Press, 1984), 21.

Bachelard picks up the wax example in an extended discussion of scientific method as a means to understanding. The fleeting qualities of changing wax are, for Descartes, a lesson in doubt. This is true in part because he believes the goal is to discover things at their most simple—wax in its essence rather than in its multitude of material forms (for instance, candles of various shapes and sizes). Bachelard suggests the changes in scientific method now offer a means to systematically study the wax to understand it as an object, a process he labels "objectification."[9] The goal is not to understand wax in its simplest form, as an ideal substance known in the mind, but rather to understand wax in its complex reality known through experimentation in the laboratory. Bachelard walks us through the process by which the wax could be explored, including the use of microscopes and X-rays to determine diffraction patterns and crystalline structures. Bachelard concludes by countering Descartes's claim that the natural conditions we perceive with our senses—with wax or anything else—are false and misleading. Rather, he writes, "In nature the conditions of observation are confused, and all one has to do is put some order into the process in order to bring organization to the real. For science, then, the qualities of reality are functions of our rational methods. In order to establish a scientific fact, it is necessary to implement a coherent technique."[10]

In reality, then, Descartes's innate truths have no place in science; rather, science is a project of verification.[11] The work of science, building on Bachelard's non-Cartesian epistemology, always takes the form of "active empiricism," or to put it another way, it "actively seeks its complex truths by artificial means."[12]

9. Gaston Bachelard, *The New Scientific Spirit*, trans. Arthur Goldhammer (Boston: Beacon, 1984), 167.
10. Ibid., 171.
11. Ibid., 12.
12. Ibid., 171. Bourdieu writes, "I tried to transpose into the field of the social sciences a whole epistemological tradition represented by Bachelard, Canguilhem, Koyré. . . . That tradition, which cannot easily be labeled with an 'ism,'

Bachelard constructs his "artificial means" by the strategic use of three key concepts—obstacles, breaks, and couples—each crucial to Bourdieu's adoption of his framework for social science.

Epistemological Obstacles

Bachelard views science as an experimental practice rooted in careful investigation. A major move here is from construing science as a progressive unfolding of reason to specific and local cases of reason. Philosophy of science depends on history of science and the careful study of fits and starts in its development in what he called "regions of rationality."[13] Any careful historical study of science shows obstacles standing in the way of a new or better understanding of reality. The most obvious obstacle is simply our commonsense understanding. Bachelard's example here is from trying to teach science to students. They assume that because a body floats, the body must be buoyant rather than the fact that the buoyancy is created by the upward resistance of the water in relation to the object.[14] Further, the wax example above shows the way Descartes's metaphysical commitment to idealism prevents him from actually exploring the objective features of wax through experimental method. One must overcome this obstacle in order to find a new approach. Such an inquiry-driven approach expects obstacles to knowledge and accounts for them. Science, Bachelard argues, makes a friend of error, seeking not "the true understanding" but *truer* understanding. Thus it does not assume what we know is true but seeks truth—or greater truth—through scientific method.

has as its common basis the primacy given to construction. The fundamental scientific act is the construction of the object" (Beate Krais, "An Interview with Pierre Bourdieu," in Pierre Bourdieu, Jean-Claude Chamboredon, and Jean-Claude Passeron, *The Craft of Sociology: Epistemological Preliminaries* [Berlin: de Gruyter, 1991], 248).

13. Gaston Bachelard, *Le rationalisme appliqué* (Paris: P.U.F., 1949), chap. 7.

14. I draw here from the excellent dissertation on Bourdieu by Daniel F. Pilario, *Back to the Rough Grounds of Praxis* (Leuven: Leuven University Press, 2005), 181.

Epistemological Breaks

If scientific work hits obstacles, science must also have means to overcome such obstacles. Bachelard calls these overcomings "ruptures" or "breaks." The first and most fundamental move of science is to break with the illusion of immediate knowledge. Bachelard's successor in his chair at the Sorbonne, Georges Canguilhem, wrote, "No one had previously devoted as much energy and persistence as Bachelard to asserting that science is constructed against the immediate, against sensations, that 'primary self-evidence is not a fundamental truth,' that the immediate phenomenon is not the important phenomenon."[15] The simple example given above relates to how one explains a body floating in water. One must break from such immediate knowledge to discover that the upward resistance of the water creates buoyancy. Another simple example, Bachelard notes, is the chemist's comment regarding the similarity between glass and zinc sulfide, which have no overt similarities at all but are similar because of their parallel crystalline structures. A break from the surface observation regarding their dissimilarities opens the possibility of seeing their molecular similarity.

A break or rupture can also occur in dramatic ways when older scientific conceptions give way to new proposals. Copernicus's formulation of a heliocentric model of the universe is perhaps the most famous example of such a break, and to Bachelard's point, Galileo's confirmation and defense of Copernicus was facilitated by the development of a new technique: the refracting telescope as an instrument for observation. Science develops not only by its break from ordinary commonsense experience but also by critical engagement with the development of tools and techniques for research.

A final kind of rupture or break Bachelard developed relates to a self-critical stance on the part of the researcher. His insistence

15. Georges Canguilhem, excerpt 1 in Bourdieu, Chamboredon, and Passeron, *Craft of Sociology*, 83.

on three levels of vigilance opens up the distinctiveness and subtlety of this break. First, the scientist is vigilant regarding the unexpected, as any disciplined and curious researcher should be. Second, however, he or she needs to be vigilant about the proper use of the methods drawn upon in this or that experiment or inquiry. Vigilance here ensures careful deployment of the processes of research. Nothing yet will seem extraordinary to those familiar with science. Bachelard introduces a novel idea when he turns to the third level of vigilance: what he calls the "monitoring of monitoring" function. This happens "when one monitors not only the application of one's method, but the method itself."[16] At times Bachelard refers to this methodological break as a technique for the "psychoanalysis of reason," which allows for unearthing the personal and social unconscious or semiconscious structures of thought one embodies unreflectively because of one's formation in particular traditions of science.[17]

Epistemological Couples

Finally, in developing his approach to science, Bachelard seeks to draw into dialectical relationship what are often seen as oppositions. His key term for these oppositions, "couples," hints at his aim: "realism and positivism, continuity and discontinuity, rationalism and empiricism."[18] He argues that science is in need of new principles, among them a view of things as dialectically complementary. One outcome of his effort to hold opposing terms in dialectical tension is what he called *rationalisme appliqué*, or applied rationalism. Applied rationalism is a mode for overcoming these dichotomies. In this, Bachelard seeks to

16. Bachelard, *Rationalisme appliqué*, cited in excerpt 2 in Bourdieu, Chamboredon, and Passeron, *Craft of Sociology*, 89.

17. I learned much from Gary Gutting's chapter on Bachelard and Canguilhem in his *Michel Foucault's Archaeology of Scientific Reason* (Cambridge: Cambridge University Press, 1989).

18. Pilario, *Back to the Rough Grounds*, 183.

"use theoretical conceptions not as abstractions from the full reality of objects but the way of reaching this reality beyond the vagueness and incompleteness of our sense experience."[19] As Bachelard scholar Mary Tiles puts it, clarifying a possible misreading of his intention, applied rationalism allows "an account of empirically (materially) engaged reasoning, not of theoretical reasoning subsequently applied."[20] To escape Descartes's idealism, Bachelard turns to empirical investigation but holds on to the commitment of idealism to the mind's active role. Thus he rejects the classic division between theory and application, between idealism and empiricism, requiring "the necessity of incorporating conditions of application into the very essence of the theory."[21] Both Bourdieu and Wacquant build on this, setting theory in practice and practicing theory as means of investigating human action with their concept of *habitus*.

Bachelard's contributions far outrun my brief sketch of some of his important ideas, yet in highlighting these I foreground those most influential on Pierre Bourdieu. We will see this in a clearer light in chapter 4. Here, however, it is enough to say that the remarkable insights Bachelard offers begin to turn science from its youthful arrogance, its dream of reason as both unitary and universal. Through his critical appropriation and revision of the Cartesian legacy, he opens up a humbler and more realistic understanding of how science works as well as how to work at science.

Sin and Self-Critique

One might say that from a theological perspective, Bachelard points out the sin of pride within science and leads it to a humble

19. Gutting, *Michel Foucault's Archaeology*, 30.

20. Mary Tiles, "What Does Bachelard Mean by *Rationalisme Appliqué?*," in *Radical Philosophy* 173 (May/June 2012): 24.

21. Gutting, *Michel Foucault's Archaeology*, 31.

repentance. As with our lives before God, this more humble, modest science is also likely truer, more fully what it was intended to be but could not be on account of its self-imposed unreality. Similarly, as we saw in the last chapter, Rowan Williams's first implication of mission framed by the practice of dispossession is to take with great seriousness the church's brokenness and humility as it faces the world.

Sin, Williams argues, is simply "living in contradiction to the purpose and direction of the universe as its maker intends it."[22] By virtue of God's very identity as divine self-giving and our being created in God's image and likeness, we *ought* to live a peaceful life of mutual love and self-giving. Instead, we are caught in a tangle of wrong turns that send us inward, toward our own desires and dreams. We can't live untruthfully, "against the grain," so to speak, without consequences. This "ingrained habit of turning in upon ourselves" becomes the only way we know how to be human, something we cannot undo on our own, and something ultimately damaging to ourselves and to the world.[23]

While we are not able to break the habits of self-absorption and self-abnegation to which sin condemns us, we sense it could and should be different when we see a glimpse of mercy, of utter self-giving. Such a glimpse may come through a person or a work of art—say, a film or a play, or perhaps even a song such as U2's "Bad." Too often, glimpses of hope are squelched by the powerful intersection of personal sin with structural sin—say, the collusions of personal convenience and corporate profit driving the fossil-fuel industry damaging our planet. We are seemingly unable to escape the cycles of desire and competition for self-aggrandizement so central to this unreality we call real.

In the old language of one liturgical confession of sin, we are in bondage and cannot free ourselves. It becomes clear, then,

22. Joan Chittister and Rowan Williams, *Uncommon Gratitude: Alleluia for All That Is* (Collegeville, MO: Liturgical Press, 2010), 52.
23. Rowan Williams, *Tokens of Trust: An Introduction to Christian Belief* (Louisville: Westminster John Knox, 2010), 82.

that something—someone—must break this cycle of sin. But who could offer a new reality recovering the true pattern of God's created intention, which takes the shape of mercy, justice, and self-giving love within a universally inclusive community? Here we see the need for Jesus. In him, we are incorporated into the "practice of dispossession" as it relates to the Trinity's self-giving in love. Dispossession, God's self-giving through the incarnation, offers the only way for a new start. How does it do this? While our rejection of Jesus follows the patterns of sin at its most violent, God's raising him to new life vindicates the reality of mercy and self-giving love over the selfish fantasies in which sin entraps us.

The parallels with Bachelard's concepts become clearer as we sketch Williams's ideas more fully. Sin presents a major obstacle to true knowledge, such that we cannot simply trust our commonsense impressions to be the truth. We must, if we seek truer understandings of the world and especially God's work in it, develop disciplined ways of asking what is going on, and these ways need to take into consideration the distorting effect of sin.

To overcome the obstacle sin presents, we need a *rupture* or *break* with our everyday blindness caused by sin's distorting power. The break comes through God's self-giving in Jesus, whose living, dying, and being raised to new life becomes an opening to our true humanity and our true life as a community before God. Jesus, by the Spirit, offers the key to seeing God and the world truly. Yet the idea of *couples* pertains here as well: we are both sinners and saints, becoming who we shall be but still struggling with the compulsions of a self-indulgent and self-abnegating sinful life. So the disciplined procedures for seeing truer understanding matter even more—they can help us love our neighbor as God loves us, seeing them as God sees us.

To really pair theological understanding with Bachelard's insights, we'll need to take one further step to show a possible example of such methodological seriousness in response to the distorting power of sin. To follow Bachelard's "applied rationalism" in theology, we need to show how the theological convictions imbue the disciplined techniques of research, or how the methods for attending to the world embody the very theological convictions that open them to truer understanding. To do this, I turn to an early exponent of fieldwork in theology, the Mujerista theologian Ada María Isasi-Díaz, in relation to a research project I'm involved in on learning pastoral imagination.

En la Lucha: Fieldwork as Theology's Self-Critique

We were sitting in a comfortable room at the lakeside retreat center. My research colleague and I were gathered with a small group of graduates of a major evangelical seminary in the southern United States.[24] We interviewed them for the first time as they finished seminary two years prior, and now in this follow-up interview we were hearing updates on their lives and ministries. L., one of the new ministers, began to tell us her story. Originally from Brazil, she, along with her new husband, also a seminarian, went back to Brazil for a "mentoring in ministry" experience during their last semester of school. She picks up the story:

> We went to work in the city where I went to college. . . . We decided to work with a very poor church in a very urban setting. They did a lot of work with homeless and prostitutes and drug addicts, so we thought that was going to be interesting. We got there and the pastor was completely against me, and J. didn't know how to speak Portuguese. I had to be involved in everything and translate, and the pastor wouldn't talk to me. That was hard. I left Brazil to come here to go to seminary because I couldn't go in Brazil. I went to seminary kind of in a dilemma because I felt the call but didn't understand how could I be called if I was a woman. It didn't make sense. Then I went to

24. This group included two blacks (one male, one female), one Latina (female), and one Caucasian (male). Both interviewers were Caucasian (one female, one male). For more see www.pastoralimagination.com.

seminary and realized I can do this, you know, women are called too, but then whenever I went into the field, I wasn't accepted. So I don't know if it was really good to learn that I was called because now I can't do anything. . . . In the church where we were working, the pastor would invite J. to come preach, go visit people in the hospital, and go to the prison with him, but I couldn't do anything, not even go with him. They wouldn't let me. . . . Once a week I was allowed to go there and wash the church, like literally wash the walls, the floor, all the chairs, wash the bathrooms, which I actually enjoyed [chuckle]. . . . At least while I was there it was like, I might just be washing the bathroom but at least it's still the house of the Lord.

In her book *En La Lucha / In the Struggle: Elaborating a Mujerista Theology*, Ada María Isasi-Díaz argues a key challenge facing Latina women is "invisible invisibility."[25] The phrase refers to the experience of being ignored by those who do not even recognize the reality of the destructive contempt they inhabit. Through L.'s powerful story of nonrecognition in her calling, we can grasp some sense of what Isasi-Díaz means. Despite her doubts about the value of theological study affirming her sense of calling when she is so utterly rejected by the church she trained to serve, washing the bathroom can be for L. tenaciously redeemed as a way to serve the Lord and as a potentially prophetic symbol of her hope to serve more fully. While consigned to clean the church as a mode of silencing, L. attempts to reframe the experience as part of her struggle not only to find her voice but also to find a place to serve in ministry.

In response to such silencing, Isasi-Díaz's Mujerista theology focuses on "the moral agency of Latinas—how we understand ourselves as agents of our own history, how we create meaning in and through our lives, how we exercise our moral agency in spite of the oppression under which we live."[26] Using

25. Ada María Isasi-Díaz, *En la Lucha / In the Struggle: Elaborating a Mujerista Theology* (Minneapolis: Fortress, 1993), 188.
26. Ibid., 2.

ethnographic group interviews as a key method, Isasi-Díaz helps create a space of attentive listening as "an opportunity for reflection" as well as "a vehicle for Latina women to develop their own voices." The research process does not aim to create theories or develop classical theological arguments but rather "to enable Latinas to grasp better their daily lives so they can more effectively struggle for survival and liberation."[27] In briefly opening up reflection on L.'s story and the mode of Mujerista theological research pitched to attend to such stories through a practice of "hearing to speech," I show a mode of theology's self-critique, naming the ways theology has ignored the very particular suffering of Latina women and building a methodology fitted to empower and dignify them in and through research. Behind Isasi-Díaz's work are two of her mentor-teachers whose work informs her approach even as she creatively develops it for her own needs.

First, Christian feminist ethicist Beverly Harrison sets a frame for channeling a righteous anger at injustice, at the social impact of what Isasi-Díaz calls "invisible invisibility." In her influential essay "The Power of Anger in the Work of Love," Harrison presents a dire picture of our common human future. Our trouble, she argues, is a societal neglect of our "most human and most valuable and the most basic of all the works of love," which she describes as "tending the personal bonds of community." Such work has been denigrated as "women's work," but its deep social power animates her vision of God's love for us and for the world. It is "through acts of love," Harrison writes, "what Nelle Morton has called 'hearing each other into speech'—we literally build up the power of personhood in one another."[28]

27. Ibid., 88.
28. Beverly Wildung Harrison, *Making the Connections: Essays in Feminist Social Ethics*, ed. Carol S. Robb (Boston: Beacon, 1985), 12. I take it as an encouragement and as a goad that Harrison wrote, "It is, I submit, urgent that men join women in doing feminist moral theology—that is, acting to keep the power of relationship alive in our world" (21).

Harrison does not mean to personalize rather than politicize the work of love; Morton was explicit about this both in claiming "hearing to speech" as political work and in describing with care its empowering effect.

Second, then, Morton, a distinguished civil rights activist and feminist theologian who was Isasi-Díaz's colleague at Drew University, offers a method adaptable for empowering research. It was Morton who popularized the phrase "hearing to speech." During a women's retreat Morton led in 1971, a woman was struggling to name her experience and did not tell her story until the end of a week together. When she finally was able to speak, this is what Morton says happened:

> When she reached a point of the most excruciating pain, no one moved. No one interrupted her. No one rushed to comfort her. No one cut her experience short. We simply sat. We sat in a powerful silence. The women clustered about the weeping one went with her to the deepest part of her life as if something so sacred was taking place they did not withdraw their presence or mar its visibility. The woman's response to this was equally remarkable, "You heard me. You heard me all the way. . . . I have a strange feeling you heard me before I started. You heard me to my own story. *You heard me to my own speech*."[29]

Morton believed the embodiment of God's redemptive love was at work in hearing another.[30]

Yet Morton knew our capacity for holding a redemptive silence is sometimes more than we can bear. She relates a circle in which the woman speaking, clearly in pain, crying, and struggling to find words, was interrupted. "Suddenly, the woman next to her turned to the woman on the other side of her and with her hand on her knee interrupted as she asked, 'P____, you have two children also. Do you ever feel that way? Tell

---

29. Nelle Morton, *The Journey Is Home* (Boston: Beacon, 1985), 205.
30. Ibid., 41.

us about it.'" It turns out the woman who interrupted was in training to be a counselor, and her newfound knowledge about helping overwhelmed her ability to simply be present and go with the first woman "down all the way." Morton relates that she could hardly "bear the pain of having the grace a woman pleaded for intercepted by women who could not go through the pain of hearing another into the depths of her own abyss where sound is born."[31] The sound, the voice, the speech being born here, while oblique, has the sense not just of human agency but also of God's agency bringing to life a new creation where estrangement and brokenness reigned.

In fact, Isasi-Díaz's work as a Mujerista theologian draws on ethnographic group interviews as a means to "hear into speech" silenced Latina women. Ethnography is preferred as a means for this theological work because it seeks to "'learn from people, to be taught by them,' rather than just gathering information about them."[32] Rather than describing their lives and circumstances, it "presents the understandings and opinions of [Latina] women, as much as possible, in their own words."[33]

Isasi-Díaz, like U2's work in the song "Bad," constructs sympathetic narratives of social suffering, seeing those whom society might judge, or even discard, as instead beloved by God. The very process of making space for another's story to be heard is a way to "break" from the self-centeredness of sin and instead hear another "as God hears."

31. Ibid., 205–6.
32. Isasi-Díaz, *En la Lucha*, 84.
33. Ibid., 66.

3

Embodied Perception

Merleau-Ponty and the Incarnate Body

Maurice Merleau-Ponty's influential work on the phenomenology of embodied perception comes in the form of a formidable tome of some seven hundred pages. Yet crucial aspects of Pierre Bourdieu's work, such as his central concept of *habitus*, would be unthinkable without Merleau-Ponty's elaboration of the incarnate body's capacity to inhabit a world just as naturally and unconsciously as it wears a garment.

A Prelude from Esperanza Spalding: "Freedom Jazz Dance"

Esperanza Spalding, a twenty-six-year-old virtuoso bassist, singer, and composer, cohosted the "Pre-Grammy Telecast 2014," which is when the bulk of the less prestigious awards are given. She cohosted with Bobby McFerrin, himself a virtuoso vocalist and conductor as well as ten-time Grammy winner.

Walking out to begin the telecast, McFerrin checked his mic, Spalding picked up her bass, and they launched into an inventive and fun version of the Eddie Harris tune "Freedom Jazz Dance," made famous by Miles Davis on his 1967 album *Miles Smiles*.[1] Spalding and McFerrin begin with a firm yet measured groove but explore a dynamic range and emotional breadth marked by intensity. Their interrelated improvisation of embodied communal jazz joins them to the band behind them and the audience in front of them.

Later that evening, much to her and most people's surprise, Spalding won the award for "Best New Artist" over teen pop icon Justin Bieber and hip-hop star Drake. As she took the stage in disbelief, she began by saying, "Thank you to the academy for even nominating me in this category." She thanked all her friends, family, and teachers, a community she described as "such a blessing" in her life and music.

Growing up, Spalding explored jazz but also played bass and sang in a popular Portland indie rock band, Noise for Pretend. Her musical range and range of interests are enormous. One report lists her iPod collection at eleven thousand songs—from Johann Sebastian Bach to Stevie Wonder. It is enough music to play continuously for nearly two months. Her range of influences match her iPod collection, causing some critics to describe her work as unfocused and too broad in style.

Others describe her eclecticism as particularly fitting as a representative of a post–hip-hop generation. Her very identity, rooted in having an African American father and a Mexican/Native American mother, embodies a kind of multiracial and multilingual complexity fitting for the internet-driven, twenty-first-century global music scene of which she is now a leader.[2] Her paired albums make the point. *Chamber Music*

1. See the song at https://www.youtube.com/watch?v=17lpfvyWhhM.
2. John Colapinto, "New Note: Esperanza Spalding's Music," *The New Yorker*, March 15, 2010, 32–39. Colapinto visited her in her Austin, Texas, home and filmed her talking about her creative process working on a new song. It is incredible to

Society (2010) employs classical depth and enhanced string ar-rangements (done by Spalding herself). *Radio Music Society* (2012) is a decidedly populist move, including originals along with spirited covers of Stevie Wonder's "I Can't Help It" and Wayne Shorter's "Endangered Species." A look at her playing schedule shows the same range; she has toured with jazz lu-minary Joe Lovano's Us Five group and opened for a series of concerts by Prince in New York and Los Angeles. The spirited nature of her music is rooted, she says, in a similarly dynamic understanding of God, "whose beauty, presences and effect in and on my life invokes infinite inspiration, admiration and wonder."[3] As she "incarnates" this divine energy, she becomes one with the music and her instruments—both upright bass and voice—and also with the song and its relational world. She is passionately reaching out, calling for response—a response those in the audience are unable to withhold.

From Spalding to Merleau-Ponty

The passionate embodiment of music and lyrics in Spalding's performance—and in most every masterful performance, whether in music, theater, film, or dance—lends itself to a dis-cussion of Maurice Merleau-Ponty's understanding of how embodied selves inhabit their world. Our bodies are not sim-ply objects in the world, something we consider objectively as we might an upright bass or a microphone, but rather are our very means for relating to and living meaningfully in the world. Merleau-Ponty made a brief appearance in chapter 1. As you recall, Michel Foucault divides French philosophy, plac-ing Bachelard on the side of philosophers of knowledge and

hear her say and show a humility that knows "sometimes a musical idea comes to me that I don't have the maturity to fully realize yet," http://www.newyorker.com/online/blogs/goingson/2010/03/video-esperanza-spalding.html.

3. Esperanza Spalding, *Junjo* (Ayva Music, 2006), liner notes.

rationality, with Merleau-Ponty representing the other side, the philosophers of experience, sense, and the subject. In order to dig more deeply into Merleau-Ponty's thought, I'll unfold a four-part discussion. First, I will note his relation to the classic problem of epistemology, especially the French Cartesian tradition Bachelard also sought to counter. Next, I'll highlight his proposal of subjectivity as essentially embodied or incarnate being. Third, I'll connect the relation of this embodied subjectivity to a world it inhabits, what Merleau-Ponty, following Martin Heidegger, calls being-in-the-world. Then, fourth, these previous points lead to a distinctive view of human knowledge and action, including a particularly distinctive view of freedom.

Overcoming Epistemology

Merleau-Ponty was both shaped by and deeply critical of the French Cartesian tradition he inherited. Its epistemological picture frames the possibility of relations with the world known through representations of it within one's mind. In grabbing hold of objects as ideas—that is, having inner representations of an outer reality—one confirms a grasp on reality. With Merleau-Ponty, "this view has been completely turned on its head."[4] Following philosopher Charles Taylor's lead, we can see Merleau-Ponty's basic moves for accomplishing this "overcoming."[5] Our grasp of the world is not, it turns out, based on such inner representations of outer reality. Rather, things make sense to us as we encounter them in our everyday activity. Such understanding, further, is not merely "my" understanding but a social reality, part of my shared world of meanings and relations. So as I encounter the door to my office, my chair, desk, and books, these are not first of all objects but things

4. Charles Taylor, *A Secular Age* (Cambridge, MA: Belknap, 2007), 558.
5. Charles Taylor's classic article in this regard is "Overcoming Epistemology," in *Philosophical Arguments* (Cambridge, MA: Harvard University Press, 1995), 1–19.

having significance to me as I inhabit my world. I can, with some focus, stand back to contemplate these *as* objects, but this is on the basis of a primary engagement with the range of things making up the everyday world I inhabit.[6]

This seemingly simple paragraph encapsulates nearly the whole drama of Western philosophy since Plato. It sets up a discussion of Merleau-Ponty's place in this drama, and especially his key idea of the "primacy of perception."[7] Drawing from his reading of Edmund Husserl's later work (and that of Husserl's most distinguished student, Heidegger), Merleau-Ponty describes persons not as pure consciousness (contemplating the range of objects visible to them) but as beings who exist in a particular world among the many objects that make up a world. Phenomenology, then, is *a way to pause and notice how it is that one has a world*—it is, in his view, a particular "manner" or "style" of thinking.[8] Whereas Descartes's procedure of doubt led him to name the essential aspect of a human being as a *cogito*, a "thinking thing" or "mind," Merleau-Ponty claims a "cogito, an 'I' or 'self' can only exist in relation to a situation, involving both a world of things and of other people."[9]

Incarnate Subjectivity

Involvement with a world necessarily means a unity of mind and body. Early in his career, Merleau-Ponty wrote a review of Gabriel Marcel's *Being and Having* for the Catholic journal *La vie intellectuelle*. He found what was to become one of his

6. Taylor, *Secular Age*, 558–59.

7. Maurice Merleau-Ponty, *The Primacy of Perception* (Evanston, IL: Northwestern University Press, 1964), 13: "The perceived world is always the presupposed foundation of all rationality, all value and all existence. This thesis does not destroy either rationality or the absolute. It only tries to bring them down to earth."

8. Ibid., lxxi: "Phenomenology allows itself to be practiced and recognized as a manner or as a style."

9. Here I've learned very much from the excellent overview by Eric Matthews, *The Philosophy of Merleau-Ponty* (Montreal: McGill-Queen's University Press, 2002), 33.

central ideas: "consciousness of self as bound to a body, as incarnate."[10] Unusual for philosophers today, he worked with the fields of physiology, psychology, and psychiatry to develop his non-dualistic ontology and his claim that our subjectivity is not distinct from our embodiment in the world.

Merleau-Ponty turns to the simple example of a blind man with a cane to show this embodied "oneness." When one becomes adept at its use, the cane extends the perceptual reach from the hand to the tip of the cane. Traditions of intellectualism, he says, would argue the blind man constructs the world of objects through the sensations of his hand, produced by the pressure of the cane on it. This is surely not correct, however, and he argues instead that "the cane is no longer an object that the blind man would perceive, it has become an instrument with which he perceives. It is an appendage of his body, or an extension of the bodily synthesis."[11] The development of perceptual habit literally gives one a world, and its direct, meaningful, and mostly unconscious relation to the world defines what Merleau-Ponty means by his phrase, borrowed from Heidegger, "being-in-the-world."

Being-in-the-World

Being-in-the-world is a phrase attempting to name our direct, meaningful, and unconscious relation to our surroundings. Critiquing the mistake of treating the world, society, and all its aspects as objects, Merleau-Ponty claims we "must return to the social world with which we are in contact through the simple fact of our existence, and that we inseparably bear along with us prior to every objectification."[12] He does not deny an

10. Gabriel Marcel, *Being and Having*, trans. Katharine Farrer (New York: Harper, 1965), 10.
11. Maurice Merleau-Ponty, *Phenomenology of Perception*, trans. Colin Smith (New York: Routledge, 1962), 153–54.
12. Ibid., 379.

objective stance, such as the distancing of the scientific gaze. He merely makes it secondary to our primary being-in-the-world. The real relationship of social agent and world is of mutual possession. "The interior and the exterior are inseparable. The world is entirely on the inside, and I am entirely outside of myself." Such interpenetration of self and world makes possible the largely unconscious yet artfully coordinated actions of daily life, something as simple as my using the door to enter the room. As I reach for the door as the way into the room, I do not need to stop to notice the door as distinct from me, as an object separate from me. In one fascinating example, Merleau-Ponty describes a soccer game:

> For the player in action the soccer field is not an "object," that is, the ideal term which can give rise to a multiplicity of perspectival views and remain equivalent under its apparent transformations. It is pervaded with lines of force (the "yard lines"; those which demarcate the penalty area) and articulated in sectors (for example, the "openings" between the adversaries) which call for a certain mode of action and which initiate and guide the action as if the player were unaware of it. The field itself is not given to him, but present as the immanent term of his practical intentions; the player becomes one with it and feels the direction of the goal, for example just as immediately as the vertical and horizontal planes of his own body. It would not be sufficient to say that consciousness inhabits this milieu. At this moment consciousness is nothing other than the dialectic of milieu and action. Each maneuver undertaken by the player modifies the character of the field and establishes new lines of force in which the action in turn unfolds and is accomplished, again altering the phenomenal field.[13]

Obviously, in order to have a world in the way this soccer example suggests requires many years of training and socialization,

13. Maurice Merleau-Ponty, *The Structure of Behavior* (Boston: Beacon, 1976), 168–69.

a reality Merleau-Ponty imagines as a basic fact of being human within a particular, concrete society.

Freedom's Constraint

The soccer example above nicely portrays the character of our last point—namely, that for Merleau-Ponty, freedom is constrained not by some arbitrary external force but by the very fact of our having a world. Borrowing from his longtime colleague and friend Jean-Paul Sartre's famous quip that we are "condemned to be free" (meaning we must choose how to be in the world given our radical freedom as human beings), Merleau-Ponty retorts that our being-in-the-world condemns us to "meaning" or "sense."[14] We are free, but only within the bounds of the meaning we are given from a soccer field and the social rules of the game learned within the context of our social life. This embodied knowing is what allows us to act easily and effortlessly, mostly without thinking in a conscious way as we navigate daily life. To add a dimension of time to the constraints on freedom, Merleau-Ponty describes the weight of a past that is present within us as "sedimentation" of experience.[15] This is true not only for the social rules of a game, such as soccer, that we learn over time, but also in terms of psychological and physiological traits we live with over time. "It is unlikely," he writes, "that I would in this moment destroy the inferiority complex in which I have been complacent now for twenty years. This means that . . . this past, if not a destiny, has at least a specific weight, and that it is not a sum of events over there, far away from me, but rather the atmosphere of my present."[16]

---

14. Jean-Paul Sartre, *Being and Nothingness*, trans. Hazel E. Barnes (New York: Washington Square, 1992), 186. In *Phenomenology of Perception*, the old (Smith) translation has "condemned to meaning" (xxii) whereas the new (Donald A. Landes, 2012) translation says, "condemned to sense" (lxxxiv). In either case the obvious target of his comment is Sartre.

15. Merleau-Ponty, *Phenomenology of Perception*, 466.

16. Ibid., 467.

Freedom's constraint as a way to demarcate Merleau-Ponty's view of the incarnate body and its immediate perception of and interaction within a world are just the theoretical framework necessary to make sense of Esperanza Spalding and Bobby McFerrin's performance of "Freedom Jazz Dance." It is not their song; she and McFerrin are working not only within the constraints of their formation as jazz musicians who are technically excellent on their instruments (vocal and bass) but also within the bounds of Eddie Harris's original composition. Much of what they do is conscious to an extent: they know that they are playing, with whom, what song, and so on. Yet the moves they make are not conscious decisions at this moment and the next, but rather a flow of preconscious action directed by their grasp of the complexity of the moment. Much like Merleau-Ponty's soccer example, the jazz playing is a summary image of "incarnated subjectivity."

Incarnation and "the One"

The direction of the chapter thus far has had theological overtones. One could suggest that Descartes's more disengaged and disembodied idea of knowledge was rooted in a wrongheaded idea of God as also disengaged and removed.[17] Instead Rowan Williams, whose work I now turn to, argues for an orthodox theology of God's self-revelation in Jesus, the incarnate Word of God, who becomes flesh and dwells with us. In rejecting the distancing move of Descartes and the disembodied, objective point of view his theory of knowledge depends on, Merleau-Ponty clearly channeled this kind of theological understanding

17. While Descartes did not coin the phrase "Watchmaker"—that was William Paley, somewhat later—Descartes did say God created the world in a rational way and its orderliness, its rationality, was the "Maker's Mark" in us and creation. Both allow us to be "like God" (rational) and to discover the laws of nature and of humanity.

and built on it an understanding of knowing as incarnated subjectivity. Humans are concretely grounded as being-in-the-world. To explore these theological implications, we build on the previous chapter's acknowledgment of sin and the consequent blindness of our everyday, commonsense understanding. We observed the need to break from such sin and blindness by finding a technique or practice of inquiry that leads to truer understanding. Theologically, such a break is given as a gift in Jesus, simultaneously the fullness of and possibility for true being-in-the-world.

I now turn to a theological account of God becoming flesh and living among us, what in doctrinal terms is called the *incarnation*. Let me start in a bit of a roundabout way by turning to Rowan Williams's little-known but powerful book of sermons, *A Ray of Darkness*, especially the sermon that gives the volume its name.[18] We saw in the last chapter that sin distracts us with false knowledge. Williams quotes the fifth-century mystic Dionysius, who used the phrase "ray of darkness" to describe the way the light of Christ appears to us in the midst of our blind fantasy of ourselves as the center of the universe. Rather than a comfort, Jesus as the "Word made flesh" dwelling among us brings on a "kind of vertigo" in which "the first thing I know is that I don't know, and never did." So the first thing to say about incarnation is that it is rooted in the pure, loving, and creative self-giving of God, who reveals this to us as the character of our true identity. In the midst of our sin, this coming is disruptive, very strange indeed. So strange, in fact, that the world "loved darkness rather than the light" (John 3:19) and killed Jesus rather than undergoing the radical transformation his incarnation invited. Yet the depth of God's self-giving mercy and love overcomes our darkness, our violent rejection of Jesus, and offers to those who can receive it (the poor in spirit) the good news that we are not condemned but forgiven, accepted,

18. Rowan Williams, *A Ray of Darkness* (Boston: Cowley, 1995), 99–104.

and invited into a new reality of communion and love with God. Jesus is both "ray of darkness" and "light of the world," both disruption and assurance, both cross and resurrection.

This is less a *doctrine* of the incarnation than a depiction of the impact of a *person* whose life we encounter and are thus changed. Williams writes, "We don't get to know what God is 'like' in the abstract; we don't get a definition delivered in the language of ideas. We get a life that shows us what God wants to happen, one that makes it possible for what God wants to become real in and for all of us."[19]

There are several important implications in this statement. First, God's creative act is fundamentally the act of self-giving. Here Williams links the *kenōsis* of Jesus as a proper act of God's character. Because Jesus's life, death, and resurrection—in sum, his "giving away" of his life for the world—brings about a new creation, "we learn to see God's creative act as in itself a giving away, a letting go."[20] In receiving this life of Jesus among us, we not only learn the nature of our true humanity as made in God's image and likeness (Gen. 1:28), but we are incorporated into this life. It is possible for us to live similarly self-giving, loving lives.

Second, as a means of clarifying the classical orthodox claim that Jesus is at once fully human and fully divine—that in his self-emptying he acts as a bridge from God to humanity and the world—Williams turns to a musical analogy. When you see a great performer, Williams argues, you see a human fully expressing his or her creative energy and potential. The video of Esperanza Spalding and Bobby McFerrin bringing to vibrant life the song "Freedom Jazz Dance" portrays this so well. Here, Williams writes, "is someone who is completely themselves, free and independent, and yet for this time, the whole of their being, their life, their freedom, their skill, is taken up in this mysterious,

19. Rowan Williams, *Tokens of Trust: An Introduction to Christian Belief* (Louisville: Westminster John Knox, 2010), 9.

20. Rowan Williams, *On Christian Theology* (New York: Blackwell, 2000), 234.

different thing that is the work to be brought to life."[21] This, he argues, is what we Christians try to say regarding Jesus as a human being—he performs God's love, God's self-giving mercy, fully and without pause. In the fullness of his performance, another is made present. So it is one person living out two lives, two "natures," but one life lived in and for the world.

Third, the fullness of this performance of God's self-giving for us opens a possibility of our being who we are created to be in the image of God, creative like God, self-giving toward our neighbors. The foot washing in John 13 is paradigmatic of our being drawn into the life and action of God.[22] If we remain in our state of fantasy, of ego inflation that turns us in on ourselves, we are blind to the truth of ourselves as creatures. Humility can as easily become a source of pride as willful arrogance. Both can demarcate the territory of sin and separation from God. Yet in receiving the gift of God's coming to dwell with us in Jesus as offense, as a "ray of darkness," we can be converted to the world and dwell in real communion with those in need. Williams especially draws out the parables and teachings that portray Jesus as particularly concerned with the one who is sick, hurt, or somehow on the margins. To these we are particularly called, fulfilling our humanity by giving away our best possessions and abilities for the sake of those who need just such gifts in community.

Sedimentations of Sectarianism: Fieldwork as Theology of the Body's Unconscious

All of this opens up theological grounding for a robust embrace of Merleau-Ponty's view of phenomenology as a "style of thinking" that takes as its starting point an "incarnate subjectivity."

21. Williams, *Tokens of Trust*, 74.
22. Benjamin Myers, *Christ the Stranger: The Theology of Rowan Williams* (New York: Bloomsbury, 2012), 75–76.

It is a critical turn in research that attends carefully to how we live as embodied creatures and to what we learn by specific attention to the character of our embodiment. As an example of such work, I turn now to Irish theologian Siobhán Garrigan. Her work attends carefully to embodied realities, both showing our ability to misrecognize violence in our embodied practice and, through specific means of attending to incarnate subjectivity, finding a way to see potential for the transformation leading to the peaceful practice God desires for us. In Garrigan's study of worship in Ireland, she asks the question of whether embodied worship practices contributed to sectarianism and violence. She thinks so, arguing that "sectarianism, like racism and sexism, works 'behind our backs' keeping us from the deeper changes of hearts and minds that would lead to 'real peace'" (as her title has it).[23] Changes of hearts and minds require careful attention first to what we are doing and the effect this has in sabotaging our peaceful goals, and then changing our practices to embody those aims we most hope for our future. A few preliminary points about Garrigan's argument are in order before turning to her case study of Irish Catholic eucharistic practice, which she considers at length in relation to the problem of sectarianism. Sectarianism may be defined as mere differences in denominational beliefs, but these beliefs are embodied over generations in an attitudinal matrix that extends through politics, economics, and the whole of life. Therefore, the Good Friday Agreements achieved civic and political peace, but the deep and pervasive structure of sectarianism's embodiments—especially seen in terms of segregation—remains.

Garrigan focuses on worship as a way both to understand these embodiments of sectarianism and to imagine means to overcome them. She is not arguing that patterns of Christian worship are the primary cause of sectarianism. Rather, noting

23. Siobhán Garrigan, *The Real Peace Process: Worship, Politics and the End of Sectarianism* (London: Equinox, 2010), xv.

that "what human beings do with their bodies sometimes betrays what they do with their thoughts," she argues that how we ritualize together as Christians embodies aspects of our basic beliefs about the world in general. Therefore, worship can embody and enact sectarianism.[24] Drawing from the work of Nicholas Healy and others, she attempts a critical theological ethnography of Irish worship practices aimed at developing a practical-prophetic ecclesiology capable of resisting destructive political realities.[25] In carrying out this ethnographic work in twenty-eight diverse congregations, she notes that her "most important research tool was my own body in the spaces being studied."[26] Aiming at uncovering practices that "work below the level of human consciousness," she took as a starting place that "one can only research ritualizations from within a body that is acted upon and configured in its subjectivity."[27]

Garrigan focuses a significant part of her study on the Eucharist as a case study in worship and sectarianism. She does this because, she says, "the fact that no congregant in any of the Roman Catholic churches studied received the cup demands considerable attention." She describes the typical pattern of parishioners proceeding up to the altar area where a priest or eucharistic minister waits to place a host ("a small, thin, round wafer which has been consecrated") into the open mouth or cupped hands. Thus receiving, the parishioners return to their seats. While not receiving the cup during communion has a long history in Western Christianity, a history Garrigan sketches, the post–Vatican II reintroduction of the Eucharist has resulted in a nearly universal return to communion "under both kinds," as the *Catechism* puts it.[28] Yet despite specific encouragement

24. Ibid., 25.

25. Ibid., 33; Nicholas Healy, *Church, World and the Christian Life* (Cambridge: Cambridge University Press, 2000), 185.

26. Garrigan, *Real Peace Process*, 32.

27. Ibid., 32–35.

28. *Catechism of the Catholic Church* (Washington, DC: USCCB, 1997), 1390.

by the Catholic hierarchy and an Irish bishops' report on the matter that encouraged catechesis and renewed practice, across Ireland the practice of reception of the host alone has endured. Garrigan came to understand this practice as an example of the "elision of 'Catholic' with 'Irish,'" in that deep-seated folk perceptions stretching back hundreds of years hold "that 'The Protestants, they receive the wine. We do not.' And in some quarters, even: 'If we received the wine, we'd be just like the Protestants.'"[29]

Not content with simply accounting for this non-reception of the cup as a simple case of sectarian differentiation, Garrigan dug deeper to discover that people's perception of communion was almost entirely mystical. "Communion is adored precisely because it is not quotidian, because it is of God's own world." It turns out that much of the post–Vatican II teaching regarding the renewal of communion treats the sacrament as a meal, an emphasis that exists at some distance from Irish Catholic understandings. To account for the deep-seated cultural aversion to seeing communion as a meal, as an issue related to eating and drinking, Garrigan considers some cultural history. The long legacy of British oppression—including the Great Famine that decimated up to a quarter of the population during the nineteenth century, but also the legacy of British portrayal of the Irish as drunks, less intelligent, and so on—contributes a grim political layer to issues of eating and drinking. Added to this is the history of resistance via hunger strikes that have included iconic deaths as part of the Republican protest against British hegemony in Ireland. In such a context, the symbolic resonance of the host as Christ's sacrifice for us can give meaning to the hunger strike as a cruciform sacrifice for the people.[30]

All this leads Garrigan to wonder, drawing on William Cavanaugh's study of the church in Chile, whether ecclesiology

29. Garrigan, *Real Peace Process*, 122.
30. Ibid., 141.

determines if "the Body of Christ is just one more body created
by the state in its own image for its own purposes." That is, she
reads the continued non-reception of the cup as a complex and
mostly unconscious continuation of a practice that nonetheless
works as a perpetuation of the very sectarianism the meal coun-
ters in its declaration of a new peace in the one body of Christ.[31]
In order to reform this practice of the Eucharist among Irish
Catholics, something like her critical theological ethnography is
needed. Without "varied, non-streamlined, context-dependent
theologies of the Eucharist," it seems unlikely that reform could
happen so that Irish people could "drink from the cup, safely."[32]

31. Ibid., 146.
32. Ibid., 147.

4

Practical Logic

Bourdieu and the Social Art of Improvisation

> Pierre Bourdieu's sociology of practice is often regarded as either too simple or too complex—either reduced to one useful idea taken out of context or disregarded as hopelessly difficult to comprehend. This chapter offers an accessible overview, beginning where he did: working on empirical studies. Starting with Bourdieu in the field, we can more easily show how his interrelated methods and concepts arose and work in concert to understand the world—and change it for the better.

A Prelude from Arcade Fire: "Wake Up"

Arcade Fire, a seven-member indie rock band from Montreal, has been critically acclaimed since their beginnings a decade ago. The 2010 album *The Suburbs* was nominated for the most prestigious of all the Grammy Awards, "Album of the Year."

They surprised everyone by winning over such megastars as Lady Gaga and Detroit rapper Eminem. Their win left award presenter Barbara Streisand looking confused, seeming to think the band's name was "The Suburbs" and the album called "Arcade Fire." Upon hearing their names called, the shocked band expressed jubilant thanks and then declared, "We're going to play another song 'cause we love music!"[1]

Indeed, part of their distinctive mark on the music scene is instrumental virtuosity—in a typical hour-and-a-half concert they will play acoustic guitar, drums, bass guitar, piano, organ, violin, viola, cello, double bass, xylophone, glockenspiel, French horn, accordion, harp, mandolin, and even on occasion a hurdy-gurdy, better known as a wheel fiddle. As if this weren't unusual enough for a rock band, they typically switch instruments over the course of their passion-fueled live shows, with no one member playing the same instrument throughout. This high-energy musicianship translates into an infectious feeling in their live performances, drawing audiences into a musical and lyrical experience of shared communal joy. One of the most extraordinary examples of this came at the Southern California Coachella Festival in May 2011. The band closed their main set with the song "Wake Up" from their first full-length album, 2004's *Funeral*. "Wake Up" is a powerful song, arresting and cajoling the listener to wake up by sheer force of its musical energy. Let me say a bit more about the band before returning to this song.

Led by the husband-wife duo of Win Butler and Régine Chassagne, who met while in college in Montreal, Arcade Fire had a number of early configurations of players before settling on

---

1. In a typically ironic yet prophetic move, they dove into the song "Ready to Start," with its biting first lines "If the businessmen drink my blood / Like the kids at art school said they would." Of course, the Grammy audience is overflowing with the businessmen and women who run corporate media and would love to have Arcade Fire on their roster, on their terms. Instead, Arcade Fire is on the roster of a small independent label, Merge Records, based in Durham, North Carolina.

a dynamic group of seven (they add a few more regular players when they tour). Win, a Texan, learned to play on a guitar
given to him by his big-band–leader grandfather, Alvino Rey.[2]
Régine, who grew up in an expatriate Haitian family living
in Montreal, was in college before she began playing music
(playing recorder in a medieval music group). Through 2003,
in fits and starts, the two were joined by an experienced group
of musician friends. Richard Reed Parry and Sarah Neufeld
were playing in Bell Orchestre, while Tim Kinsbury and Jeremy
Gara were playing with Parry in the New Internationals. Win's
younger brother, Will, got involved while on break from college,
and the band was set. The combination of challenging ideas,
musical virtuosity, and passionate performance has made the
band a live favorite and sparked their rise over the last decade.

Described as "a scholarly post-punk gospel choir merrily
identifying the menace of the world," the band shares a unique
combination of art, music, and politics.[3] The brothers (Win and
Will) and the husband-wife duo (Win and Régine) help ground
this communal orientation. Régine says, "Our togetherness is
what makes us special. It's what feeds into the music, and I think
people can feel that, that it is important to us because it is our
life, not just our career."[4] Despite Régine and Win writing most
songs, the band shares credit for songwriting and arranging, an
acknowledgment of their communal work ethic and commitment to equality. The communal nature of the band has also
translated into the band's commitment to support Régine's
homeland of Haiti. They have actively worked against the ex-
treme poverty of that island nation, especially in the wake of
the devastating earthquake of January 2010.

    2. Michael Barclay, "The Arcade Fire: Talk about the Passion," *Exclaim.ca*,
September 2004, available at http://exclaim.ca/Features/OnTheCover/arcade
_fire-talk_about_passion.
    3. Paul Morley, "Keep the Faith," *The Guardian*, March 18, 2007, http://www
.guardian.co.uk/music/2007/mar/18/popandrock.features11.
    4. Ibid.

Since 2010, Régine and Win, along with others in the band, have spent time in Haiti volunteering with Partners in Health, an organization the band has supported from early on. They dedicate a dollar from every ticket to every concert and have raised millions of dollars for work in Haiti. They have consistently been ambassadors for Haiti, speaking to audiences in support of relief and development aid. As a witness to the ongoing struggle for basic needs in Haiti, Win plays an acoustic guitar with the words "*Sak vide pa kanpe*" written in large duct tape letters on its front. In English, it means "an empty sack cannot stand," a Haitian proverb evoking the devastating impact of poverty.

Arcade Fire's songs open up avenues of reflection on some of the issues that matter most in life—whom we serve with our lives, how we live and love, what we create with the gifts we have been given, and what is worth fighting for and against. Their depth of passion as musicians is driven by their passion for ideas, including the core idea that life is to be lived fully, awake, and with deep concern for the lives of others, whether it be their fellow band members, their fans, or the poorest people in the world today. All of this exuberance is channeled into their live concert performances, exemplified by the Coachella festival performance mentioned above. As their main set closed, Win belted out, "This is our last song, so I want you to sing it really loud." The insistent drum and violin signaled the song "Wake Up," a crowd favorite, and within seconds tens of thousands were singing along with the band at the top of their lungs. Suddenly, large bouncing balls came pouring over the top of the stage, becoming a huge mass of bouncing joy throughout the crowd. But then, almost in sync with the band, the orbs began to glow in blue, purple, pink, red, green, and violet, and the energy that had peaked at a roar rose a few notches more. The faces of the band were clearly caught up in the joy of the moment, a communion of immense proportions that seemed to be the fully realized

possibility of rock 'n' roll concerts to take people outside
of themselves. Their passionate performance reimagines the
festival so that it becomes possible to lose oneself in time in
a kind of effervescent flow—without thinking at all about
it—yet knowing this is life in all its fullness.

Arcade Fire launches our engagement with Pierre Bourdieu
on a couple of levels. Most directly, his core pair of concepts,
habitus and field, help us understand the practical, embodied
mastery of a band like Arcade Fire as well as the complex
roles of the audience and the whole corporate world behind
the promotion and consumption of music today. In addition,
Arcade Fire's clarity about the power of the market to shape
the lives of bands and their self-consciousness about their
own position of power and influence turned toward the suffering in Haiti connect with Bourdieu's own commitments
to social justice and the exposure of causes of social suffering
and oppression.

From Arcade Fire to Bourdieu

In the opening chapter of this book, I rehearsed the two main
misunderstandings of Pierre Bourdieu, first as a theoretician's
theorist and second as a social determinist. Both are misguided,
as I began to show already in that chapter. In order to more
fully ground an understanding of Bourdieu's key themes while
further dismissing these misunderstandings, I turn to a discussion of the impact of his early work in Algeria. After noting
his commitment to an ethical and political social science (he is
not a social determinist) and his practice of sociology as a craft
(he is not merely a theorist), I explore how the problems arising
from fieldwork forced the development of theoretically informed
concepts for use as tools in research. These concepts function to
overcome typical antinomies in social science and philosophy,
most importantly between subjectivism and objectivism.

The Influence of Algeria

First, Bourdieu's apprenticeship or initiation into social science after being trained in philosophy occurred because of an ethical concern—that is, a feeling of solidarity with the social suffering of ordinary Algerians during his military service in the Algerian War of Independence (1954–62).[5] He was conscripted for military service, beginning as a guard at a major munitions storage facility but then via transfer served as a clerk for the French administration in Algiers. During weekends and evenings he began research on a small book intended "to tell the French, and especially the people on the left, what was really going on in a country of which they often knew next to nothing—once again, in order to be of some use, and perhaps also to stave off the guilty conscience of the helpless witness of an abominable war."[6]

After this foray into social research, he fully intended to return to philosophical work, but "rooted in a kind of passion for everything about this country, its people and its landscapes, and also in the dull but constant sensation of guilt and revolt in the face of so much suffering and injustice" he found himself drawn more and more deeply into the labor of understanding this place and people.[7] This moral concern, so passionately expressed here, constitutes the drive to develop an approach to research Bourdieu calls "socio-analysis," a "collective counterpart to psychoanalysis" that makes possible destroying the "myths that cloak the exercise of power and the perpetuation of domination" (and therefore opens avenues for political change).[8] Perhaps recalling his work in Algeria, Bourdieu writes,

5. Pierre Bourdieu, *Sketch for a Self-Analysis* (Chicago: University of Chicago Press, 2008), 59.
  6. Ibid., 40.
  7. Ibid., 47.
  8. Pierre Bourdieu and Loïc Wacquant, *An Invitation to Reflexive Sociology* (Chicago: University of Chicago Press, 1992), 49–50.

The idea of a neutral science is a fiction, and an interested fiction, which enables one to pass as scientific a neutralized and euphemized form of the dominant representation of the social world that is particularly efficacious symbolically because it is partly misrecognizable. By uncovering the social mechanisms which ensure the maintenance of the established order and whose properly symbolic efficacy rests on the misrecognition of their logic and effects, social science necessarily takes sides in political struggles.[9]

Here one sees the ways his view of science maintains "an intellectual posture which leads to conceive the work of the researcher as an activist task (and conversely)."[10]

However, Bourdieu, while clearly eager to have his work aid in political struggles, does not think the proper role of science is directing political change. Here he differs from those "total intellectuals" like Sartre who used their prominence to lead political movements (even Foucault, whom he greatly admired, fell in this category), valuing instead a deep commitment to collaborative research and scientific discipline. Yet even here, throughout his life, and especially in the last decade, Bourdieu was willing also to be a citizen and speak in newspaper editorials or small books about issues of great contemporary concern.[11] He rarely did this as a lone voice, however, preferring to make joint statements and build a "collective intellectual" voice similar to his desire to work collaboratively in his social science research. Along these lines, Bourdieu founded a "collective" to oversee a book series titled Raisons d'agir (Reasons to Act), designed to offer works of social science to a broad public in accessible form and inspired by an activist desire to spark political discussion. He contributed the best-selling *On Television* himself as an

9. Ibid., 51.
10. Ibid., 58.
11. Many of Bourdieu's political writings of this sort have helpfully been collected in a posthumous volume. See Pierre Bourdieu, *Political Interventions: Social Science and Political Action* (New York: Verso, 2008).

inaugural volume, hoping to spark critical perspectives on the
role of media in contemporary society.[12]

Second, his self-described passion for understanding, combined with a distinct lack of training in social science and especially fieldwork (remember that he trained in philosophy), led
him to think in fresh ways about how to solve practical challenges in fieldwork as a craft. He developed research methods
and concepts to further develop the craft of research. He drew
upon his philosophical background for help, a reason for his
friendly adoption of British philosopher J. L. Austin's phrase
"fieldwork in philosophy" to describe his approach.[13]

At the time, Lévi-Straussian structuralism was on the ascen-
dency with *The Elementary Structures of Kinship* appearing in
1948 and, to great acclaim, *Tristes tropiques* a few years later.
At first Bourdieu found structuralism quite useful, but as I
will explain more fully below, the confrontation with the daily
social world of his subjects forced him beyond the structuralist
paradigm. An ethical concern drove his critique of Lévi-Strauss,
whose position as researcher implied "the haughty and distant
relationship established between the researcher and the object
of his research, namely ordinary people." Whereas structuralism made the agent into "a mere 'bearer' of the structure,"
Bourdieu "insisted on asking the informants the question
why."[14] His own "apprenticeship" in fieldwork, during which
he learned alongside colleagues from the University of Algiers
and developed new research practices as needed, led him to
view fieldwork as a craft, albeit one of disciplined scientific
work. To teach it, he argued, is to "have more in common
with a high-level sports coach than with a Professeur at the
Sorbonne." One teaching the craft of research "looks very

12. Pierre Bourdieu, *On Television*, trans. Priscilla Parkhurst Ferguson (New
York: New Press, 1999).
13. Pierre Bourdieu, *In Other Words: Essays toward a Reflexive Sociology*
(Stanford, CA: Stanford University Press), 28.
14. Ibid., 20.

much like a coach who mimicks a move ('if I were you I would do this') or by 'correcting' practices as they are executed, in the spirit of practice itself ('I would not ask this question, at least not in this form')."[15]

Fieldwork and Concept Development

Out of Bourdieu's commitment to the use of science for social understanding and even political intervention, it was necessary to develop concepts that allowed for getting very close to the reality of social life as it is lived. Here we see Bourdieu building a mode of scientific work grounded in fieldwork. Precisely because of the problems he confronts in the field, he must therefore overcome antinomies such as objective/subjective and social/mental. His core concepts (some might say theories, which is not wrong but needs to be understood in the right way—that is, never disconnected from their use in particular theoretically informed research projects) of *habitus* and field, along with others, emerge at just this juncture. Many discussions of Bourdieu go wrong by separating his theory from his method and separating both from their emergence from concrete programs of research, something attentive readers will notice Bourdieu never does. While many points along his very productive career could serve our purposes here, it was his fieldwork in Algeria that was most formative and over which he labored the longest. I'll draw here from the preface of what is regarded as one of his best and most important books dealing with his fieldwork in Algeria, *The Logic of Practice*.[16]

15. Bourdieu and Wacquant, *Invitation to Reflexive Sociology*, 224.
16. *The Logic of Practice* is in fact the third version of his effort to write this book about his fieldwork in Algeria. The first was published as *Esquisse d'une théorie de la pratique, précédé de trois études d'ethnologie kabyle* in 1972. Bourdieu totally rewrote the book for its English version, *An Outline of a Theory of Practice* (Cambridge: Cambridge University Press, 1997). He again rewrote and rearranged the book for *Le sens practique* (Paris: Minuit, 1980); English ed., *The Logic of Practice* (Stanford, CA: Stanford University Press, 1990).

Bourdieu begins by noting the overwhelming influence of Sartre and Lévi-Strauss as he struggled to make sense of his years of fieldwork in Algeria. The whole preface is in one sense an account of his overcoming of the powerful influence of dominant schools of academic thought influencing the study of peasant society. Bourdieu's interest in rituals partly emerged from Lévi-Strauss's collecting of descriptions of rituals of all sorts, cataloged by type and placed within comprehensive systems to portray their logic. In this process, local variation drops out and essential types or aspects are cataloged within local patterns. The "structure" or "model" provides a set of "rules" presumably governing the unconscious operations of social life.

Yet Bourdieu and his research partner, Abdelmalek Sayad, continuously ran up against "countless contradictions" to their models. The formal logic of the structure fit the actual diversity of practice only very roughly and with necessary disregard for variation. In fitting daily patterns to the agrarian cycle as part of the mythic ritual system, for example, they found the loom is to weaving as field is to corn and woman is to child. Each distinct ritual—domestic craft, agriculture, or reproduction—can be fitted to this overall logic in the structuralist paradigm. But the logic here is, borrowing from medieval sacramental theology, the logic of *opus operatum*. The work produces itself, or to place the logic within its medieval context, the mere act of performing the sacrament produces the grace conferred. Bourdieu eventually rejected this logic. The model does not describe the actual logic of ritual practice; rather, Bourdieu argues, the ritual practice has its own *modus operandi* (its own way of working). In an excellent description of what would be lost if practice were in fact to happen *opus operatum* as Lévi-Strauss and the structuralist position argues, he writes,

> If practices had as their principle the generative principle which has to be constructed in order to account for them, that is, a set of independent and coherent axioms, then the practices

produced according to perfectly conscious generative rules would be stripped of everything that defines them distinctively as practices, that is the uncertainty and "fuzziness" resulting from the fact that they have as their principle not a set of conscious, constant rules, but practical schemes, opaque to their possessors, varying according to the logic of the situation, the almost invariable partial viewpoint which it imposes, etc.[17]

So, for example, one can produce a lexicon of practice showing *that* funeral chants are sung by men at harvest time and by women when cloth is being cut from the loom. But this does not help one in understanding the particular instances of actual practice. Bourdieu came to desire ways to understand not the formal logic of the structure of mythic belief and ritual action but the actual practical mastery of it by those who inhabit the practices. It amounts, Bourdieu writes, to his "becoming ill at ease with the definition of the object that structuralism offered when, with a confidence to which I could not aspire, it asserted the epistemological privilege of the observer."[18]

In another example, Bourdieu describes an effort to study patterns of marriage that were, according to previous ethnographic studies of the Kabyles people, typically between parallel cousins. He noticed, however, that the patterns of marriage were poorly explained by simply claiming they were variations of the rule of parallel cousin marriage. When someone married outside their tribe, a major ceremony was held, whereas within a family, as with parallel cousins, a simple ceremony sufficed. Drawing on Max Weber's notion of material interest, he began to see these differences not merely as variations of a formal rule governing marriage but rather as dimensions of social strategy deployed within a larger system of social and economic life.[19]

17. Bourdieu, *Logic of Practice*, 12.
18. Ibid., 14.
19. Ibid., 15–17.

To make progress, then, Bourdieu argues one has to "bring into scientific work and into the theory of practices that it seeks to produce, a theory which cannot be found through theoretical experience alone—of what it is to be 'native,' that is, to be in that relationship of learned ignorance of immediate but unselfconscious understanding which defines the practical relationship to the world."[20] However, he is quick to point out the native is not just the Algerian peasant but any person seen from the perspective of the fuzziness of the practical strategies by which he or she navigates daily life.[21] "Social agents, in archaic societies as well as in ours, are not automata regulated like clocks, in accordance with laws which they do not understand."[22] Using the analogy of a game for the various domains of social life, Bourdieu suggests people acquire a generative *habitus*, a system of dispositions giving them a feel for the game and enabling an infinite number of moves within the bounds of the game. Developing this concept of *habitus* was the bridge from rules to strategy, a means to acknowledge that many "types of behavior can be directed towards certain ends without being consciously directed to these ends, or determined by them."[23]

These fieldwork experiences have brought us to the point of the emergence of concepts Bourdieu created for the sake of deeper understanding. I'll say a bit more about the especially crucial pair, *habitus* and field. Both concepts demarcate sets of relationships. Field is a way to name objective, historical relations within a specific domain of society, sports for example, while *habitus* similarly names these same relations deposited like sediment within one's embodied capacities of perception and action, as in the soccer player. Their pairing draws from both the objective (structuralist) pole and the subjective (existentialist) pole but doesn't fall prey to the limits of either. The

20. Ibid., 19.
21. Ibid., 20.
22. Bourdieu, *In Other Words*, 9.
23. Ibid., 9–10.

agent is neither a puppet on strings nor totally autonomous, but rather has limited freedom within the framing structure of the field. One could imagine this like a soccer field, with its bounds and positions and goals, its ball and rules of play both limiting and making possible kinds of action for players. Those who have the requisite experience can engage in the game on the field as the space for the structured possibilities of the game. The *habitus* replicates the sense of the game and its variety of possible plays literally *within* the players, who are embodied and available as improvisational repertoire. Bourdieu puts it simply: "The body is in the social world but the social world is in the body."[24]

Another example from Bourdieu's fieldwork will likely make this clearer. In the "religious field," Bourdieu carried out a study of French Catholic bishops. He interviewed a range of current bishops from ages thirty-five to eighty. While the field structures the "game" of being a bishop similarly in terms of its "highness, distance, and separation" from the everyday people of faith, bishops who came of age in the provincial town of Meaux tended to come from noble descent and would ask the worshipers in their parishes to kiss their ring, an ecclesial holdover from feudal aristocratic shows of loyalty. Younger bishops from the leftist working-class suburb of Saint Denis were so-called red bishops, active in social justice work and siding with those who suffer.[25] *Habitus* and field, then, are always a "historically constituted, institutionally grounded, and thus socially variable, generative matrix."[26] These bishops are at play in the same game, within the same structure of formation and institution, but the contours of the game change over time as do the patterns of formation of those who join in the game.

24. Bourdieu and Wacquant, *Invitation to Reflexive Sociology*, 18.

25. Ibid., 135. See Pierre Bourdieu and Monique de Saint Martin, "La sainte famille. L'épiscopat français dans le champ du pouvoir," *Actes de al recherche en sciences sociales* 44/45 (1982): 2–53.

26. Bordieu and Wacquant, *Invitation to Reflexive Sociology*, 19.

Drawing together this set of reflections on Pierre Bourdieu's work, try this exercise to see how culture shapes us, how it forms the assumptions we make, the way we see the world, and therefore the actions we imagine are possible and reasonable. Write down (or make a mental note of) your response to the following picture. Take a minute to really look at it and let your responses come to some clarity.

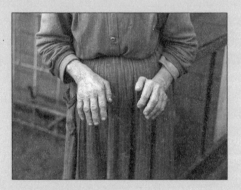

What came to mind as you looked at this picture? When Bourdieu did this experiment as part of his famous study of class and aesthetics published as *Distinction*,[a] he found that those from a higher socioeconomic class (and who were likely also more urbanized) were interested in the photo as a beautiful if painful metaphor for age or life's difficulty. Those with closer proximity to the hard labor of the working class felt visceral horror at the deformity of these hands and commented about the actual difficulty of a life of hard labor. The point is that who we are, how we were raised, the sorts of families, schools, and so on, that formed us shape our cultural sensibilities and frame how we live—the assumptions we make, the actions we see as possible and appropriate, and so on. Culture consists in objects not just "out there" but also "in here," as I discussed with Merleau-Ponty in chapter 3. The material life of which we are part and parcel shapes our outlook, our *habitus*.

a. Pierre Bourdieu, *Distinction: A Social Critique of the Judgment of Taste*, trans. Richard Nice (Cambridge: Cambridge University Press, 1984), 36–37.

The concepts of *habitus* and field additionally show how Bourdieu advocates the fusion of theory and method—they are theoretically defined concepts created as tools for fieldwork. Here he pushes not only against a divide in sociology among those who do "theory" and others who do "empirical research" (and always, within the games of sociology, valuing the theorist more highly) but also against the practical suggestion that one does research and then develops theory. Instead, theory is practical in that it frames and forms the very dispositions, the *habitus*, of the researcher in the process of research.[27] This disciplined stance is drawn directly from Bourdieu's training by Bachelard and Canguilhem, discussed in chapter 2, especially in terms of the construction of the object through theoretically informed empirical research. Research tools fitted for the character of the investigation should always be used, and a critical stance toward the process of construction itself—the "break" required from "common sense" leading to a point of view more attuned to understanding (more) fully—should be adopted.

To take the discussion of the *habitus* of the researcher one step further, let me add here Bourdieu's term "reflexivity." It is not a concern unique to Bourdieu, but his use of it is distinctive and absolutely crucial to his understanding of research. It is, first of all, not an individual term but something he thinks bears on the collective nature of science in general; the practice of scientific research should be self-critical (*re-flectere* means to bend back). Bourdieu focuses most directly on three sorts of reflexivity. First, the social location of the researcher introduces influences that must be accounted for. Second, the social space within the academic field occupied by the researcher must also be accounted for. Third and most subtle—but also most important because of that—is the intellectualist point of view, the temptation of the academic to view the world as an object and create for oneself a "God's eye" view in relation to it. This is, in a way, the problem

27. Ibid., 35.

Bourdieu first saw in relation to Lévi-Strauss's structuralism. The danger is thinking the theoretical picture we produce is actually the true reality of those we seek to understand—as if the map were the way people navigate the neighborhood.

While this chapter can only begin to open up the breadth and depth to be found in the diverse research and writing across Bourdieu's half-century career, in fact this whole book is meant to be a fuller introduction to his world and work. Even so, the limits of what I have discussed here are glaring, and I feel the lack keenly even as I turn now to discuss the connections that might be drawn to ecclesiology.

Concrete Church

As we turn from Bourdieu's social science to theology, we might expect a certain impatience with idealist construals of the church and the Christian life. The reference to his study of bishops above ought to make that clear. Presumably Bourdieu would be glad to read Rowan Williams's claim that the theologian cannot begin work from an abstract place but rather in the middle of the action of life. Williams writes,

> There is a practice of common life and language already there, a practice that defines a specific shared way of interpreting human life as lived in relation to God. The meanings of the word "God" are to be discovered by watching what this community does—not only when it is consciously reflecting in conceptual ways, but when it is acting, educating, or "inducting," imagining, and worshiping.[28]

Given such an opening claim regarding theological method, one would think that Williams would sooner or later turn to

28. Rowan Williams, *On Christian Theology* (New York: Blackwell, 2000), xii.

fieldwork of some sort. At least that is what Nicholas Healy argues. In response to Williams, Healy questions this theological method of "always beginning in the middle of things."[29] The claim, Healy writes, that the meaning of God is to be "discovered by watching what this community does" reflects the turn to practice in modern theology. This is particularly true with respect to the philosophy of Wittgenstein, whose work on language, practice, and forms of life presupposes such a method. In order to take Williams's proposal a bit further, Healy suggests, one would immediately be faced with having to "make decisions about the 'what' and the 'how.'" We will need to make decisions regarding "just what 'this community' is that we are to watch: Is it the church as a whole or just a part of it; if a part, which part?" Then, in addition, Healy notes, we must ask "how we should watch it, with what agenda in mind and with what approach."[30]

Turning to various ethnographic studies of churches to develop his argument, Healy makes three very interesting points. First, he argues that persons in community, and individual persons within communities, hold inconsistent or even incoherent views regarding God and the Christian life more broadly. This is not simply to make the obvious point that quite different Christian congregations (Pentecostal and Roman Catholic, for example) differ dramatically in their beliefs and practice. A second point is that communities and persons within the same tradition (Roman Catholic, for example) also differ in substance of belief and patterns of practice, such that they might seem unlikely to fit within the same community or even to worship the same God.[31] This pertains, Healy argues, even when one looks at belief and practice within one congregation.

29. Ibid.

30. Nicholas M. Healy, "Ecclesiology, Ethnography, and God: An Interplay of Reality Descriptions," in *Perspectives in Ecclesiology and Ethnography* (Grand Rapids: Eerdmans, 2012), 182.

31. Healy draws on the very interesting study of Catholic congregations by Jerome P. Baggett, *Sense of the Faithful: How American Catholics Live Their Faith* (Oxford: Oxford University Press, 2009).

Third, Healy notes that the diversity of belief and practice does not simply emerge from a congregation's life together. Rather, it is dispersed in everyday life in the wider community and impacted by varied nonchurch people and their practices, attitudes, experiences, and so on. The net result of these three points derived from ethnographic studies (although the implications for theological method are obviously Healy's) is to claim that Williams's approach—that is, to look for coherence and consistency among the members of a given congregation in order to know the meaning of God—is misguided. Or it is at least likely to be inconclusive, since Healy's argument leads him to the conviction that the church is called to be "the world's Christian expression." To put it differently, he thinks the distinctiveness of the church will be hidden because the true distinctiveness "lies outside ourselves, in God and in the world."[32]

Healy has, I think, gotten very far down a road we need to travel if we wish to develop an approach to something we might call "fieldwork in theology." If Williams does not yet follow his own method in the ethnographic direction Healy hopes he will, his reflections on church are, indeed, worth exploring in more depth, as the empirical evidence in the church's practice might not be what Healy was expecting. Williams's claims, in fact, relate directly to the argument of this book thus far and in this chapter on Bourdieu in particular: it is a critical moral claim about *how* we look at the church or at any other social reality and about the *impact* of how we look on what we are able to see there.

The opening claim about theological method Williams offers is that a theologian begins in the middle of things and begins to say something about God through the common life and language already there and being practiced as a specific way of life in relation to God. Therefore, what the community does helps us know the meaning of "God" within that community.

32. Healy, "Ecclesiology, Ethnography, and God," 199.

Williams himself puts "God" in quotes, presumably with full knowledge that this will be a complex answer. While it is not everyone's cup of tea, what might be most helpful to my argument is Williams's chapter "Trinity and Ontology," which engages Donald MacKinnon's writings on idealism and realism. It spells out key features of how we look at the world and what this looking has to do with understandings of God, as well as its implications for church and the Christian life in the world. Without attempting to reproduce a quite subtle argument, I'll outline the logic in its basic moves.

Williams dives into MacKinnon's discussions of idealism and realism, a debate about how one knows anything or secures a claim about the truth of oneself and the world as it exists. It is a debate about fundamental ontology, and it has a long history in philosophy and theology. Suffice it to say that idealism has tended to have quite a disembodied claim (familiar already in our discussions of Descartes above) that the individual constructs a world of things in correspondence with the picture one has of them in one's mind. MacKinnon's arguments for realism are driven by a "determination to demythologize a free, triumphant, endlessly resourceful, sovereign willing self" represented by classical idealism.[33] Understanding why this matters is crucial; it is, Williams says, the *moral* concern about realism that drives the critique.

The criticism of idealism focuses on its detached mastery of the world, often driving toward abstract essences rather than particulars, which entails unavoidable loss—that is, tragedy or suffering loses its sense. Williams returns again and again to claims regarding the primacy of practical reason, to a conviction that "we cannot think away particulars into comprehensive explanatory systems; the world is such that attention to particularity is demanded of us."[34] Some views of God follow the trail

33. Williams, *On Christian Theology*, 154.
34. Ibid., 155.

of idealism, and Williams calls them out on their tendency to make God into a cosmic organizing principle or an abstract postulate. Baldly put, Christians must begin to answer the question of God's identity via the particularity of Jesus. Idealism and its portrayals of God, therefore, are not only potentially immoral in that they can overlook the "is-ness" of suffering and tragedy but also profoundly un-Christian in that they cannot account for the particularity of Jesus and the suffering of the cross.

As an alternative, Williams argues, we have knowledge of God because of the particularity of Jesus; that is, knowing God "begins by repeating the story of Jesus."[35] This is the case because of a particularly paradoxical argument regarding the way God becomes human—God is constitutively significant for Jesus's identity. It is not that Jesus is so "like" God that his whole being points to God. No, that is not enough. God is what is *distinctive* about Jesus's identity, a "putting at risk" of God's unity by "grounding within the eternal the essentially human element of temporality."[36] We have no other language for the unity of God but this story of risk lived in Jesus. We, in fact, cannot say what God is in God's essence save what we can say by the narrative of Jesus's life, death, and resurrection. The point is that we do not begin with the Trinity, asking about the being and action of God as God's self. Rather, we begin "in the world of particulars, cross, empty tomb, forgiven and believing apostles." *Kenōsis*, then, is defined not only as the earthly form of Jesus's life (John 13), but self-giving love is the very life of God as well.

Williams connects this careful christological work to a claim about the importance of tragedy, of pain in the world that seems unjustified, undeserved, and also unavoidable. This is not fatalism—rather, it is an acknowledgment not only of human limit but also human experience: "Tragedy resists the

35. Ibid., 156.
36. Ibid., 158–59.

trivialization of experience."[37] If God indeed is fully known in and through Jesus—Jesus as God's history, so to speak—then we have secured a truthful moral vision about real suffering. For example, it aids us in facing such tragic social facts as racism, "both the suffering of victims of racism and my own *de facto* involvement in and responsibility for this."[38] Yet our seeing of God in and through the cross and resurrection bears forth the reality of reconciled relationships—those of Jesus and the disciples first of all, but us as well. We see here a new community with a distinctive sense of identity, one gained by truthful vision and reconciling relationship built on the presence and gift of God's life in Christ.

To describe the reconciling power of relationship in Christian community, Williams introduces the work of the Holy Spirit as the "divine condition for 'coming to judgment' in the Church's life."[39] God is constitutive for the life of the church in the sense that a new perception is formed in the Spirit's judgment of the church in relation to the cross of Jesus. To encounter the Spirit with Christ, Williams argues, we must encounter judgment regarding "our complicity in the cross, and so with the crosses of our own making in the present and past."[40] Such truthful judgment becomes a central component of Christian protest, empowering action while simultaneously holding the church to a life of penitence. Limits to our action are rooted in our past failures and can't too easily become utopian visions of grandeur. Protest and penitence, or truthful speech leading to humble action, mark the life of the church in the power of the Spirit. It is a complex vision, but as Williams puts it, "'Complexity as a source of resistance' is no bad summary of MacKinnon's theological project."[41]

37. Ibid., x.
38. Ibid.
39. Ibid.
40. Ibid.
41. Ibid.

Marshaling classical theological doctrine—trinitarian and incarnational—as a source for truthful action models careful attention to the particulars of Jesus's life as the way we know God; it also opens a path to truthfully facing the particularities of life together as the church in and for the world. It does not fully answer Healy's critique of Williams, in part because Williams's avoidance of ethnographic work hides the actual diversity and even incoherence of the church's unity from him. One might assume Healy is more on the side of Bourdieu, focused on carefully disciplined attention to the real rather than imposing idealist pictures of reality on it. However, I don't think theology works quite that way.

Bourdieu, as we saw above, developed ways of paying attention to daily life such that he can understand the practical logic of action. His push against idealism is matched by the development of a sophisticated set of theoretically informed tools for field research chosen and employed for specific research projects. In a similar way, Williams draws on MacKinnon's critique of idealism as a way to ground classical doctrine as a theological frame for understanding church and world in their full complexity, both in their suffering and in their hope for reconciliation. Healy is asking, I think, for Williams to do the fieldwork, or to move toward it more directly and consider the dynamics of actual churches. As Bourdieu needed the most sophisticated philosophical resources to develop the methods of fieldwork he employs in "fieldwork in philosophy," so we need the most sophisticated theological resources to develop methods of fieldwork in what we call "fieldwork in theology."

Embodied Traditions: Fieldwork as Theology of the Places of Redemption

What such sociological and theological work opens up, as both Williams and Healy argue in the end, is a focus on concrete churches, not some idealistic church without historical, everyday flesh-and-blood reality. No better example can be found for such an endeavor than Mary McClintock Fulkerson's study of a multiracial congregation in North Carolina. Employing Bourdieu and others in creative ways, she also has ample place for recognizing tragedy—especially the social harms of racism and ableism—and its effects on the church and the world in which the church lives. Fulkerson, a professor of theology at Duke Divinity School, exemplifies this turn to ethnography in her own professional evolution. Her first major book, *Changing the Subject*, drew on critical social theory to elaborate a critique of feminist theology's "universalist" claims regarding women's experience. Arguing that the "female subject" is variously constructed and plural, embodying complex and competing discourses, she seeks to "change the subject" so that such multiple subjectivities are the basis for further theoretical work on difference and identity.[42]

Fulkerson's initial work in feminist theology and social and cultural theory led to her participation in a conference at the University of Chicago in 1997 that sought to more explicitly articulate the ways theologians were turning from philosophy or the history of ideas to culture as a primary conversation partner for their work. Fulkerson brought her ideas of complexity and hybridity to the study of the culture of a local congregation, Good Samaritan, where she had done "two years of interviewing and observing participants."[43] Drawing on Bourdieu, she emphasizes the creative habituation of values of inclusion at the heart of the church's interracial identity. Yet, rather than agree on some simple movement from belief and ritual to the

42. Mary McClintock Fulkerson, *Changing the Subject: Women's Discourses and Feminist Theology* (Minneapolis: Fortress, 1994).

43. Mary McClintock Fulkerson, "'We Don't See Color Here': A Case Study in Ecclesial-Cultural Invention," in *Converging on Culture: Theologians in Dialogue with Cultural Analysis and Criticism*, ed. Delwin Brown, Sheila Greeve Davaney, and Kathryn Tanner (New York: Oxford University Press, 2001), 140–57.

formation of habits, she argues for a more open and contested notion of a "repertoire" available for the persons and community as they act out their life together.[44]

By the time of Fulkerson's book-length analysis of this congregation, published in 2007 as *Places of Redemption*, she explicitly describes her fieldwork as ethnography. She begins the book by recalling an ethnography class where she gained the fieldwork practices by which she sought to "bring something fresh to theological reflection on ordinary Christian community."[45] She doesn't aim for an "objective" analysis of the community (having, along with the postmodern anthropology she had read, given up on such an idea). Rather, she tried to do research and write in a way that was "adequate to the full-bodied reality that is Good Samaritan, one capable of displaying its ambiguity, its implication in the banal and opaque realities of ordinary existence, even as it allows for testimony to God's redemptive reality."[46]

A fascinating aspect of Fulkerson's work, her attention to tradition not as doctrinal but as communal and embodied, draws on Bourdieu. By focusing on "incorporative practices," she could seek to understand Christian community through its daily communal practices, which "convey their own meaning in the performance; contemporary bodily activity is itself the communication."[47] These practices are best gotten at, she argues, through Bourdieu's concept of *habitus*, a way of seeking to understand bodily formation and nonconscious behavior.[48] Especially regarding the centrality of issues of race and racism within an interracial church, by deploying *habitus* she could attend to bodily forms of discomfort, visceral reactions, and

44. Ibid., 147.
45. Mary McClintock Fulkerson, *Places of Redemption: Theology for a Worldly Church* (New York: Oxford University Press, 2007), 3.
46. Ibid., 7.
47. Ibid., 46.
48. Ibid., 35.

the like over against the congregation's overt language of color-blindness and full inclusion. Though some of their daily communal practices carry forward forms of exclusion, they also find redemption through a communal life offering "space to appear" for people viewed by the wider society as marginal. Arcade Fire, Bourdieu, and Fulkerson converge here: seeking to remedy social suffering through emphatic understanding, a kind of moral solidarity with those in need—be it Haiti, Algeria, or North Carolina.

5

Surrendering to the Other

Wacquant and Carnal Sociology

> Loïc Wacquant is arguably Pierre Bourdieu's most famous and most productive student. He both clarifies Bourdieu's work and extends it in creative and prophetic ways in his own engagement with issues of poverty and social suffering. His distinctive approach to the use of his own body as a research tool both depends on and creatively develops Bourdieu's concept of *habitus*. It is particularly relevant for developing fieldwork in theology rooted in the dispossession of Jesus in self-giving love for the other, the stranger, the one in need.

A Prelude from Lauryn Hill: "Black Rage (Sketch)"

I recognize the familiar tune from Rodgers and Hammerstein's "My Favorite Things," a lead song from *The Sound of Music*, within seconds. Yet from the first line, "Black rage is founded on two-thirds a person," the sample and rhyme create a prophetic

tension. The lines continue detailing the horror of mistreat-
ment of African American people—violence in blunt physical,
economic, psychological, and spiritual forms. The traditional
chorus for the song, "When the dog bites," has quite a different
resonance here. Lauryn Hill kept the line and changed the next
from "When the bee stings" to "When the beatings." Hill wrote
and began singing the song in concerts on tour in 2012 but only
released the song in response to the shooting of an unarmed
African American teen, Michael Brown, in Ferguson, Missouri,
in the summer of 2014. Brown's shooting by Officer Darren
Wilson sparked mass protests followed by brutal military-style
suppression of the protests. In her tweet upon release of the
song, Hill said, "An old sketch of Black Rage, done in my living
room. Strange, the course of things. Peace for MO.—MLH"[1]

Hill, who grew up in East Orange, New Jersey, began singing with "Pras" Michel in high school and later with Michel's
cousin, Wyclef Jean. The group eventually took the name
Fugees, recording a number of albums at the intersection of
hip-hop, R&B, and reggae. Their second album, *The Score*,
was a major success, topping the Billboard 200 and winning
a Grammy Award for Best Rap Album. Its tough depiction of
urban life, for example denouncing police brutality and corrup-
tion on the song "The Beast," is paired with a beautiful version
of Roberta Flack's "Killing Me Softly," which won a Grammy
in the R&B category. Soon after the album was released, Jean
left the group to pursue a solo career, and Hill began work on
her own solo album.

Inspired by Carter G. Woodson's famous *The Mis-Education
of the Negro*, Hill recorded a brilliant album titled *The Misedu-
cation of Lauryn Hill*, released in 1998.[2] It debuted at number
one, becoming one of the best-selling hip-hop albums ever and

1. Lauryn Hill, "Black Rage (Sketch)," song and lyrics available at http://ms
laurynhill.com/post/95329923112/black-rage-sketch.
2. Woodson is considered the father of African American history. His classic
book was originally published in 1933.

the first major album in the genre by a woman. Its theme is love, with interludes set in a classroom with a teacher (Ras Baraka, a spoken-word poet who is now mayor of Newark, New Jersey) and students discussing various aspects of love. The songs range widely in style and theme but take a distinct biographical direction, reflecting on Hill's success ("Lost Ones"), a troubled relationship with Wyclef Jean ("Ex-Factor"), and her decision to start a family during the years of recording ("To Zion"). Its first single, "Doo Wop (That Thing)" is a playful, self-effacing, yet bitingly critical take on relationships and sex that encourages young women and men to respect themselves and to see each other as more than "about that thing."

The song "Black Rage (Sketch)"—and much of Lauryn Hill's music—evokes a tradition of singing the pain of black experience in the United States going back to Billie Holiday's "Strange Fruit" and before that the "sorrow songs" of the slaves.[3] This song opens the territory within which I want to consider the work of Loïc Wacquant. Despite his background as a white French academic, and perhaps in part because of it, Wacquant has a strikingly clear and provocative angle of vision on the long-term consequences of America's "peculiar institution": chattel slavery.[4] As with Hill, though, he does not accept a position of resignation in the face of social ill but uses the tools of his craft to raise a protest, opening possibilities for living otherwise.

From Hill to Wacquant

Loïc Wacquant's formative years follow paths similar to those of his mentor, Pierre Bourdieu. Both were born in rural southern

3. For more on these traditions of African American song, see Christian Scharen, *Broken Hallelujahs: Why Popular Music Matters to Those Seeking God* (Grand Rapids: Brazos, 2011), 49–74.
4. Kenneth M. Stampp, *The Peculiar Institution: Slavery in the Ante-Bellum South* (New York: Random House, 1989).

France, sent for higher education in Paris, and began studies in disciplines other than social science; and their formative field-work experiences took place in French colonial settings marked by oppression and revolution. The similarities, however, are in some sense only happenstance; what intentionally binds them is their longtime relationship as teacher and student, mentor and apprentice, in the craft of research as reflexive social science. After an overview of his life and work, I focus in on two key ways Wacquant builds on Bourdieu's legacy: a radicalized use of the concept of *habitus* and a deep moral and civic concern for the suffering of the other.

Born in 1960 in a village near Montpellier in the south of France, Wacquant attended local schools. His success led him to Paris for study, first in management, at one of the famous *grande écoles*, the *École des hautes etudes commerciales*. While he was interested in economics, he found the professional focus on management and business to be a bad fit. In the midst of this despair, a compassionate friend took him to hear a lecture by Bourdieu not long after his start at the *College de France,* whose charter is to be a public institution with open lecture courses. He was absolutely captivated, despite not being able to fully understand, and boldly asked Bourdieu out for coffee following the lecture. They stayed up late talking, and soon Wacquant also joined a sociology program at the University of Paris Nanterre so he could pursue studies with Bourdieu. He wrote a thesis on education and reproduction, reflecting a clear influence of Bourdieu.[5]

After a brief scholarship year at the University of North Carolina working with professors Gerhard Lenski and Craig

5. The biographical information is drawn primarily from a long interview published as Loïc Wacquant, "The Body, the Ghetto, and the Penal State," *Qualitative Sociology* 32 (2009): 101–29, and a summary of the interview in article form, "Habitus as Topic and Tool: Reflections on Becoming a Prizefighter," in Anthony J. Puddephatt, William Shaffir, and Steven W. Kleinknecht, *Ethnographies Revisited: Constructing Theory in the Field* (New York: Routledge, 2009), 137–51.

Calhoun, he was sent off to a far-flung French colonial outpost—the South Pacific island of New Caledonia—for his com-
pulsory military service. Through what he regards now as an
extremely fortunate turn of luck, he was assigned to France's
former office of colonial research, ORSTOM, and was charged
with carrying out studies of the local population. As he recalls
it, New Caledonia was a nineteenth-century-style colony, very
oppressive, with a history of enslavement and radical segregation of the indigenous population called the Kanak. His first
publications chronicled these realities, including his firsthand
experience with the Kanak Uprising in 1984–85.[6] He combined
his travels with in-depth reading of the classics of ethnology,
especially those written about the South Pacific islands. Of
particular importance was Bronislaw Malinowski, whose work
in the nearby Trobriand Islands is viewed as a founding classic
of modern anthropology.[7]

Near the end of his military service, Wacquant received
a four-year PhD fellowship in sociology to the University of
Chicago. His direction emerged by virtue of being given the
last available graduate student apartment on the very edge of
Woodlawn, a so-called ghetto neighborhood in south Chicago,
and the opportunity to join a research project on the black urban
"underclass" led by professor William Julius Wilson.[8] While
he was pursuing a sociological project about social marginality and urban poverty, he felt uneasy with the notions in the
popular literature, including Wilson's term "underclass." He
felt his work needed to be grounded in the lived reality, not just
a view from afar. Living "in between" the white, wealthy Hyde

6. See, for example, Loïc Wacquant, "The Dark Side of the Classroom in New
Caledonia: Ethnic and Class Segregation in Nouméa's Primary School System,"
Comparative Education Review 33, no. 2 (May 1989): 194–212.

7. Bronislaw Malinowski, *Argonauts of the Western Pacific* (New York: Dut-
ton, 1961).

8. This project led to Wilson's important work *The Truly Disadvantaged: The
Inner City, the Underclass, and Public Policy* (Chicago: University of Chicago
Press, 1987).

Park neighborhood of the University of Chicago and the black ghetto all around it helped make this direction obvious. But even here the focus could have been more observational, more sterile, with much less of a "feel" for the lived realities. After his friend took him to a boxing gym just three blocks south of his apartment, he recognized its potential as a vantage point from which to see the ghetto as a whole.

At first, Wacquant saw the Woodlawn boxing gym simply as a way to hang out, meet informants, and make progress on his project with Wilson studying the "urban underclass." Bourdieu encouraged him, "Stick it out, you'll learn more about the ghetto in this gym than you can from all the surveys in the world."[9] He did keep at it, more interested in the relationships and the exercise than in boxing. But after a year of finding himself drawn into the passion and excitement of boxing, he decided to take on the gym as both a window into the life of the ghetto *and* a distinct microcosm of the ghetto's realities. As Wacquant puts it,

> That is how I found myself working on two connected projects simultaneously—two projects ostensibly very different from each other but in fact tightly linked: a carnal microsociology of the apprenticeship of boxing as sub-proletarian bodily craft in the ghetto, which offers a particular "slice" of this universe from below and from inside; and a historical and theoretical macrosociology of the ghetto as instrument of racial closure and social domination, providing a generalizing perspective from above and from the outside.

In the midst of this research, tensions arose and riots broke out in poor suburbs of major French cities and other European nations. Public sentiment shifted in the direction of a xenophobic panic about immigrants, the poor, and the ghetto. In response, Pierre Bourdieu began a collaborative three-year

9. Wacquant, "Habitus as Topic and Tool," 143.

project documenting the difficulties of social marginality. Wacquant spent those years doing fieldwork part-time in the Quatre Mille housing project northeast of Paris.

The research in Paris and other French cities led to a major work titled *La misère du monde*.[10] It is a compilation of short stories recounting the everyday circumstances of social suffering. The interview transcriptions are the result of listening to a variety of people struggling (mostly) within French society—new immigrants, working poor, youth, and so on. Each interview had analytic introductions focused on a critique of the dominant discourse about ghettos as well as the role of the state, arguing that *neighborhood* effects turned out to be effects of the *state* inscribed in space. The book had a major impact in France, topping the best-seller lists and beginning national debates on inequality. Wacquant contributed two comparative chapters about American realities drawn from his fieldwork in Chicago and realities in the French context. In addition, during these years Wacquant worked with Bourdieu on a book introducing him to Anglo American readership and attempting to correct the widespread misreadings and distortions of his work.[11]

As Wacquant delved into life interviews with ghetto residents, especially with the boxers at the gym in Woodlawn, he soon realized nearly all of them had spent time in prison. Some cycled in and out of prison while he was at the gym. This included O-Jay, his sparring partner, who learned to box in jail and whom Wacquant bailed out multiple times.[12] This experience led to a pilot study of jails in 1998–99 in Los Angeles, Chicago, and New York (as well as Brazil). As he began research, he was shocked by what he calls "carceral hyper-inflation" and its

10. Pierre Bourdieu, *La misère du monde* (Paris: Éditions du Seuil, 1993); English translation, Pierre Bourdieu et al., *The Weight of the World: Social Suffering in Contemporary Society*, trans. Priscilla Parkhurst Ferguson (Stanford, CA: Stanford University Press, 1999).

11. Pierre Bourdieu and Loïc Wacquant, *An Invitation to Reflexive Sociology* (Chicago: University of Chicago Press, 1992).

12. Wacquant, "The Body, the Ghetto, and the Penal State," 111.

connection to shifting policy and rhetoric—in both social science and journalistic commonsense terms circulating in the public discourse about security and safety.

Following from the success of *La misère du monde*, Bourdieu and his colleagues founded the book series titled Raisons d'agir (Reasons to Act). They intended the volumes to be slim yet substantial engagements in current social and political topics. They invited Wacquant to write a volume on what he was discovering at the intersections of policing, incarceration, and social marginality. Titled *Les prisons de la misère* (*Prisons of Poverty* in English, which loses the obvious connection to *La misère du monde*), it quickly became an international best seller.[13] According to Wacquant,

> *Prisons of Poverty* [tracks] the international diffusion of the policy of "zero-tolerance" policing which is the spearhead for the penal treatment of poverty. This book was quickly translated into three, six, sixteen languages because this policy of punitive containment of the precarious fractions of the new urban proletariat has spread across the entire globe in the wake of economic neoliberalism.[14]

Out of this set of interconnected investigations, over the past decade Wacquant has published a trilogy of similarly interconnected books: *Prisons of Poverty*, on the diffusion of "hyper-incarceration"; *Urban Outcasts* (2008),[15] which coined the phrase "advanced marginality" as a way to describe the state of urban poor globally; and finally *Punishing the Poor* (2009),[16] which asks what the state does about these "social problems" dealt with in *Urban Outcasts*. It especially points

13. Loïc Wacquant, *Prisons of Poverty*, 2nd ed. (Minneapolis: University of Minnesota Press, 2009).

14. Wacquant, "The Body, the Ghetto, and the Penal State," 112.

15. Loïc Wacquant, *Urban Outcasts: A Comparative Sociology of Advanced Marginality* (Malden, MA: Polity, 2008).

16. Loïc Wacquant, *Punishing the Poor: The Neoliberal Government of Social Insecurity* (Durham, NC: Duke University Press, 2009).

to social policies connecting what he calls the "assistential and penitential sectors" of governmental control.

Habitus *Radicalized as Carnal Sociology*

While conducting these more traditional macrosociological studies, Wacquant was drawn deeper into the Woodlawn Boxing Club as a positive space, one he intriguingly compares to a church in the sense that it provides sanctuary from the troubles of the world, but a space of intense formation as well, requiring rituals of bodily sacrifice for the sake of gaining a practical mastery of boxing as a social art and practice.[17] In order to carry out this study, Wacquant understood himself to be deploying Bourdieu's concept of *habitus* both as a topic and a tool.

Explicitly channeling Bachelard through Bourdieu, the fieldwork challenges forced innovation in research practice. The object and method of this inquiry were not of the classic mold. *Body and Soul* offers an empirical and methodological radicalization of Bourdieu's theory of *habitus*.[18] Wacquant explains,

> On the one hand, I open the "black box" of the pugilistic *habitus* by disclosing the production and assembly of the cognitive categories, bodily skills and desires which together define the competence and appetence specific to the boxer. On the other hand, I deploy *habitus* as a methodological device, that is, I place myself in the local vortex of action in order to acquire through practice, in real time, the dispositions of the boxer with the aim of elucidating the magnetism proper to the pugilistic cosmos. The method thus tests the theory of action that informs the analysis according to a recursive and reflexive research design.

17. Loïc Wacquant, *Body and Soul: Notebooks of an Apprentice Boxer* (New York: Oxford University Press, 2004), 13; he expands on these connections in an interview available at https://www.youtube.com/watch?v=v0wZjkHTLy4.
18. Ibid.

The idea behind this research agenda was to flip the standard position in fieldwork of participant observation so that it becomes observant participation.

As Wacquant recounts, the typical advice for social science researchers as they head out to do fieldwork is "Don't go native." It is a kind of warning to keep one's critical perspective and has led to a range of denials about investment and involvement in the social life one is engaged in (and impacting by one's engagement). Wacquant's position, however, went beyond typical participant observation.[19] It was less "observation" and more a throwing oneself into the life of the gym as far as possible, seeking as full a "participant" role as possible. Wacquant's advice is as follows:

> "Go native" but "go native armed," that is, equipped with your theoretical and methodological tools, with the full store of problematics inherited from your discipline, with your capacity for reflexivity and analysis, and guided by a constant effort, once you have passed the ordeal of initiation, to objectivize this experience and construct the object—instead of allowing yourself to be naively embraced and constructed by it. Go ahead, go native, but come back a sociologist![20]

The sociological aim is, to quote Bachelard, to construct a "particular case of the possible" in relation to the world under investigation—in this case the urban ghetto.[21] It is important to recognize that the central character of the story is neither Wacquant, who gained the nickname "Busy" Louie at the gym because of his slight frame and quick footwork in the ring, nor this or that boxer he trained with—and not even Dee Dee Armour, the old coach, in spite of his position as the conductor

19. Ibid., 11.
20. Wacquant, "The Body, the Ghetto, and the Penal State," 119, emphasis original.
21. Gaston Bachelard, *Le nouvel esprit scientifique* (Paris: P.U.F., 1949), 58; see also Bourdieu and Wacquant, *Invitation to Reflexive Sociology*, 75.

who orchestrates the movements of the whole. The central character is the gym as a social and moral forge. Wacquant gained proximity to the boxers' world through the gym and the boxing selves it produced by an ethnographic apprenticeship, through placing himself in the "vortex of action in order to acquire, through practice, in real time, the dispositions of the boxer."[22]

In positing Bourdieu is right that "we learn by body," Wacquant describes his work in Woodlawn as setting the course for sociology *of* the body but also *from* the body, which requires submitting ourselves to the sometimes difficult and painful apprenticeship to the other in context. Such a giving of oneself over to learn from another through the discipline of patient imitative practice forges the corporal and mental dispositions that make up the competent boxer within the crucible of the pugilist universe. A bodily submission, then, to the rigors of apprenticeship *in situ* becomes both the object and means of inquiry, opening, as Merleau-Ponty described, access to sensory-motor, mental, and social aptitudes—a corporal intelligence that tacitly guides "natives" to a particular, familiar universe.[23] It is, as Wacquant argues, a "mutual molding and immediate 'inhabiting' of being and world, carnal entanglement with a mesh of forces pregnant with silent summons and invisible interdictions that elude the scholastic distinction between subject and object as they work simultaneously from within, through the socialization of cognition and affect, and from without by closing and opening viable paths for action."[24] While the phrase "insider knowledge" begins to name what Wacquant is after here, the "knowledge" is of the sort that is both practical and habituated so its patterns become flesh and bone—my world that I inhabit as a matter of course without the necessity of

22. Wacquant, "Habitus as Topic and Tool," 7.

23. Maurice Merleau-Ponty, *Phenomenology of Perception* (New York: Routledge, 1962).

24. Loïc Wacquant, "Carnal Connections: On Embodiment, Apprenticeship, and Membership," in *Qualitative Sociology* 28, no. 4 (Winter 2005), 466.

conscious decision leading action. While boxing may be an unusual example from the perspective of most readers of Wacquant's work, he means it as a particular case of the general truth of human action. It could have easily been a corporate boardroom, a machine shop, or a local congregation.

Moral Passion and Civic Sociology

Finally, stepping back from the particulars of Wacquant's work on urban marginality, the prison, and the boxing gym as a site of incorporation into the complexity of this world, it is important to note the common ground between Bourdieu and Wacquant regarding sociology and social justice. While he does not elaborate on the influences of his family of origin that I am aware of, it is significant that Wacquant dedicated *Urban Outcasts* "To my mother, for teaching me the sense of social justice." Indeed, his depiction of his reasons for crossing over from the University of Chicago to explore the Woodlawn neighborhood, at the time 98 percent African American and very poor, was a moral one.[25] He recalls, "I deemed it epistemologically and morally impossible to do research on the ghetto without gaining serious first-hand knowledge of it."[26]

Wacquant also sees a role for sociology in agitating for social change. It is not a neutral science merely seeking objective knowledge but an engaged science seeking to clarify the causes of social injustice and the sorts of understanding that allow effective action in response. The joint development of the Raisons d'agir (Reasons to Act) series emerges from just such a motivation. Wacquant describes this approach as "civic sociology"—that is, "an effort to deploy the tools of social science to engage in, and bear upon, a current public debate of frontline societal significance."[27]

25. Lydia Lyle Gibson, "Due South," *University of Chicago Magazine* 98, no. 3 (February 2006), http://magazine.uchicago.edu/0602/features/south.shtml.
26. Wacquant, "Habitus as Topic and Tool," 141.
27. Wacquant, *Prisons of Poverty*, 161.

Like Bourdieu, however, Wacquant does not see his role as social scientist as one who claims the correct direction for policy. His activist position, his civic sociology, has a different yet significant aim in supporting social change. In an interview, he was asked directly how his research can help guide the work of activists. His answer is instructive. "That is for them to say or to discover. But activism is beset by snares and decoys which lead to a phenomenal squandering of collective energies. When that happens, one must have the honesty to say 'Stop, that is not the right issue, you are wasting your time.' That can be the role of the researcher."[28]

Going further, he specifies two key ways a vibrant civic social science can aid activism and inhabit a kind of scholarly activism itself: as solvent and beacon. First, the social sciences can make a civic contribution by acting as a solvent of the common sense circulating in the current state of affairs through the careful critique of the categories and topics that weave the fabric of the dominant discourse. He comments,

> On this front, it is a matter of giving the greatest possible number of citizens the tools for reflection needed to take back their own thought about the social world, so that they are not taught by the media, invaded by the prefabricated ideas that the latter diffuse in a steady stream, so that citizens may question the very schemata that frame political debate—and be in a position to challenge, not only the proposed solutions, but the very diagnosis of the problems that society faces.[29]

Second, social science can function as a beacon casting light on contemporary social transformations that for a whole variety of reasons may be unnoticed. A major example in Wacquant's own work is the development and diffusion of "zero-tolerance policing," which in the 1980s led to hyper-incarceration,

28. Wacquant, "The Body, the Ghetto, and the Penal State," 127.
29. Ibid., 129.

especially in the United States but also globally. Bringing these "latent properties or unnoticed trends" to light, Wacquant argues, makes their dynamics and impact clear "and especially reveals possible alternative paths, points of bifurcation in the road of history."[30]

While this chapter only sketches the richness and power of Wacquant's integrated research on social marginality, incarceration, and state security policies, I hope it is enough to make clear the multiple overlapping influences of Bourdieu as well as Merleau-Ponty, Bachelard, and others. Above all, there is a refusal to turn away from social suffering and to look deeply enough, to learn from the other well enough, to then name the contours of reality experienced by these persons who all too often are made invisible in contemporary society. It is the practice of moral attention, making visible the invisible, which hip-hop—and Lauryn Hill's song "Black Rage (Sketch)" in particular—so compellingly introduced us to at the beginning of the chapter.

Ethics and the Other

Wacquant's version of social science opens easily to theology partly because, like Bourdieu, he uses terms such as "incarnation" and "church" as reference points for realities he seeks to describe in sociological terms. Yet their theological resonance is implied, as if the ancillary depth of theological understanding helps shed light on social realities his research aims to illumine. Further, Wacquant's moral countenance toward the other is driven by a concern at once theoretical and methodological, epistemological and moral.

I'll briefly return to the practice of dispossession. Recall the practice is first and foremost a divine action, one directed

30. Ibid.

toward the whole creation in its longing for healing and new life. Because of the character of this practice and the One whose character it is to so act, the movement is toward those on the margins, as many of Jesus's parables make clear. Perhaps the most famous of these, the parables of the lost sheep, the lost coin, and the lost son (Luke 15) all portray the divine seeker whose primary concern and hope is finding and embracing the lost.[31] Yet dispossession as a practice has deeper roots in MacKinnon's work on the concept of *kenōsis*, with its most eloquent description related to divine life found in the Philippians 2 passage where "Christ Jesus, who, though he was in the form of God, did not regard equality with God as something to be exploited, but emptied himself" (vv. 5–7).

The practice of dispossession and its pattern of divine action, *kenōsis*, is grounded in and incorporates us into its movement through participation in the church's sacramental life. Baptism and Eucharist presume our condition "pre-sacramentally," so to speak, therefore anticipating and enacting God's embrace of us "while we were still sinners" (Rom. 5:8) through participation in the sacrament. Rowan Williams works out these implications, grounding our practice of dispossession in our participation in the sacraments as the foundation of our life in Christ.[32] In baptism, our very selves are given over and given back in return, stripping away our various allegiances in order that this new belonging can take root in us. In the Eucharist, our identity and mission are incorporated into the unity of Christ's own identity and mission so that, in the words of Augustine, "it is to what you are that you reply, 'Amen.'"[33] In a beautiful passage, Williams writes, "By his surrender 'into' the passive forms of

31. A particularly beautiful elaboration of this point is Miroslav Volf, *Exclusion and Embrace: A Theological Exploration of Identity, Otherness, and Reconciliation* (Nashville: Abingdon, 1996), 156.

32. For example, see his "Sacraments of the New Society," in *On Christian Theology* (New York: Blackwell, 2000), 209–21.

33. Augustine, "On the Nature of the Sacrament of the Eucharist, Sermon 272," http://www.earlychurchtexts.com/public/augustine_sermon_272_eucharist.htm.

food and drink he makes void and powerless the impending betrayal, and more, makes the betrayers his guests and debtors, making with them the promise of divine fidelity, the covenant, that cannot be negated by their unfaithfulness."[34]

To recall MacKinnon here, the point is that our security, the assurance of the meaning of our identity as persons and as Christians, is not secured by our possession of some earned status but by receptivity, by gift, by the very promise of God for us.[35]

We might speak of our formation for mission as being rooted in the very actions of Jesus, who—in presiding over our sending by the Spirit—takes us, blesses us, breaks us, and gives us over to the world's hunger. The discussion of Wacquant's carnal sociology in this chapter, then, leads me to suggest that what Williams is after with this idea of the "practice of dispossession" is something like *habitus* as a habituated, regulated improvisation that exists as part of persons formed through participation in the Eucharist. Unlike the Eucharist, the practice of dispossession is transposable from the context of the Eucharist to many everyday settings where the gospel challenges us to live *in* or *as* mission—God's mission, or dispossession—to and for others.

Embodied Theologies: Fieldwork as Carnal Theology

Such a "carnal sociology," a sociology *from* the body, transfigured into a "carnal theology" illuminates dynamics at the heart of Christian faith that one might gesture toward in a preliminary way through categories such as God's "indwelling" or, perhaps better, "incarnation." Natalie Wigg-Stevenson's work is only now emerging into wider academic and ecclesial conversations,

34. Williams, "Sacraments of the New Society," 216.
35. Donald MacKinnon, "Kenosis and Establishment," in *The Stripping of the Altars* (London: Fontana, 1969), x.

but it will be influential and deserves serious consideration here. A constructive theologian and Baptist minister teaching at Emmanuel College, University of Toronto, Wigg-Stevenson received her PhD in theology from Vanderbilt, where she benefited from the imaginative and integrative Theology and Practice doctoral program. Typical theology departments would not approve an experimental study of theological production in local congregational life, much less an ethnographic study of teaching and learning theology with laypeople in an adult church education class. Yet the multidisciplinary nature of the Theology and Practice program allowed her the dynamic intellectual space to do the year-long study, which shows the fruit of adopting Wacquant's carnal sociology for theological purposes.[36]

In some ways the project Wigg-Stevenson carried out at First Baptist Nashville has overt parallels to Wacquant's study of the Woodlawn gym.[37] In order to understand the field of theology, she not only grounded this study in actual practice—a theological class in a local congregation's adult education program—but she also included herself as a distinct and integral part of her study, consciously constructing her role as theologian and teacher. "The particular bodily dimensions of belonging" as a member, minister, and theological educator "opened up unexpected methodological possibilities" for her research.[38] She was able, as Wacquant puts it, to go beyond the ethnography *of* the body and deploy herself as topic and tool in an ethnography *from* the body.

Consequently, as with Wacquant, readers might mistakenly construe her study to be autobiography or memoir, which is decidedly not the case. Rather, the study is about the theology

36. The Theology and Practice program was analyzed in Bonnie Miller-McLemore and Ted A. Smith, "Scholars for the Church," *Christian Century*, February 26, 2008, 36–38, 41.

37. Natalie Wigg-Stevenson, *Ethnographic Theology: An Inquiry into the Production of Theological Knowledge* (New York: Palgrave Macmillan, 2014).

38. Ibid., 73.

classroom, particularly in a congregational setting. Further-
more, it is a congregational setting fraught with complicated
politics. While the congregation is a founding member of the
conservative Southern Baptist Convention, located just blocks
from the convention's national headquarters in Nashville, its
profile leans progressive, as its willingness to ordain Wigg-
Stevenson shows. So the congregations' own politics mirrored
in interesting ways the politics Wigg-Stevenson inhabits as a
minister and theology teacher. The contested politics of the
congregation allowed her space to draw upon feminist pedagogy,
which itself became a component of the class conversation about
theology and practice. The tensions around conservatism and
reform within the congregation were real tensions she and her
class had to negotiate. The example she begins the book with
makes this point—each night having to reset the room into a
circular seminar-style setup from a traditional chairs-facing-
forward lecture setup. She and her participants understood this
as part of the theological debate of the class—and the politics
they constantly negotiated within the life of the church.[39]

The congregational location was crucial for Wigg-Stevenson
to raise a major question for her study. "I was curious to see what
could happen when the goods of academic theology intervened
in ecclesial conversations so that, in turn, the goods of the
ecclesial environment might be able to interrupt conversations
in academic theology."[40] Her intentional engagement of and
attention to everyday and academic theologies in conversation
mark one of the innovations such a method can accomplish.
Typically, academic theologies are constructed in relation to an
abstract church and articulated in ideal terms.[41]

39. Ibid., 2–3.
40. Ibid., 2.
41. Nicolas Healy's *Church, World, and the Christian Life: Practical-Prophetic Ecclesiology* (New York: Cambridge, 2000) powerfully portrays this tendency in academic theology and calls for the sort of theological ethnography Wigg-Stevenson carries out here.

In some respects it was a classical theological exercise: a first semester course on Christology/Soteriology and a second semester course on the Trinity. Wigg-Stevenson brought materials from the sweep of Christian tradition past and present; the people gathered in the classroom brought their prior educational experiences, knowledge, and insight to the conversation. Her ambitious aim was not just to reflect "*on* Christian community or *on* Christian practice" but rather to attend through ethnographic means to "theological reflection *in* Christian community and *as* Christian practice."[42] Further, she wanted to find a way to do constructive theology collaboratively with laypeople whose formation as Christians and opinions about formal academic theology varied widely.

While each pursue it differently, Lauryn Hill, Loïc Wacquant, Rowan Williams, and Natalie Wigg-Stevenson each embody a posture of love leaning over toward the other and seeking to listen, hear, and understand the experience of the other. Beyond this, they articulate this experience for the sake of better naming the character of our struggles, along with whatever openings they might point toward inhabiting the world, so that we can participate in God's redemption by being present in spaces of appearing, healing, and mutually respectful connection.

42. Wigg-Stevenson, *Ethnographic Theology*.

Epilogue

Understanding as a Spiritual Exercise

Now at the end of this journey, I return to the start—the dramatic challenges facing the world and the need for the church to "wake up" (as all the songs and artists I discussed call us to do, in one way or another). The church needs to look outward and ask the challenging question of how God is at work loving the world and how we can get involved. To do so, I've argued, leaders need the capacity to understand what is going on and how to think about how God is involved with the world. The book offers an introduction to a major social scientist under whose mentoring I learned to look with discipline and understanding. That discipline and understanding surely could be gained in a variety of ways. Here I have offered it through the mode of fieldwork drawn from Pierre Bourdieu. We've been able to understand his approach more deeply by attending to formative influences on his development as well as seeing how his work developed further in the work of an exemplary student.

Bourdieu's approach to fieldwork, as you now know, is a complex craft; it includes participation, interviewing, and other research practices, along with methodological frames such as reflexivity and concepts such as field and *habitus*. Yet it is also profoundly simple and beautiful, grounded even for Bourdieu in a religious frame, making clear his openness at least to move in the direction of fieldwork in theology, even if his theology would certainly not be drawn from orthodox Christianity, as is mine.

It may be helpful to say clearly, in an extremely brief form, how each of the chapters above seeks to spell out both the "fieldwork" side and the "theology" side of the craft of fieldwork in theology. With chapter 2, we focused on the rigorous self-reflection in Gaston Bachelard's philosophy of science, connecting it to Rowan Williams's concern with the church's brokenness and humility as it faces the world. Chapter 3 engaged the embodied perception found in Maurice Merleau-Ponty's phenomenology as an entryway into a grounded, fleshly, incarnational approach to being with the world, and especially those most on the margins. The fourth chapter directly delved into Pierre Bourdieu's construal of a practical logic that helps us to avoid the trap of idealist pictures of the church and instead seeks to understand its concrete reality in communion with the world God loves. The fifth chapter picked up Loïc Wacquant's development of Bourdieu's trajectory, especially embodying an apprenticeship-to-the-other as a theoretically informed practice of field research conducive to the idea of sacramental "self-giving" to the other.

I assume you have turned to this book because a key part of your work at the moment requires disciplined effort to understand faith lived out both in community and in all the diverse settings of daily life. Bourdieu wrote reflections on understanding at the end of a 650-page book of interviews and analysis regarding social suffering. The larger work is called *The Weight of the World: Social Suffering in Contemporary Society*. His concerns include the power of the researcher and the potential for violence occur in one of those studies. He is quite adamant that researchers ponder the social gaps between themselves and those they wish to understand and how to close that social distance by "solidarity" and "sympathetic comprehension."[43]

As a shorthand way of referring to the work of sympathetic comprehension, Bourdieu calls interviewing "a spiritual exercise" insofar as researchers are invited to put themselves in the place of the interviewee.[44] However, he quickly cautions the reader not to understand by this some romantic feeling of connection (given how easily one could ignore one's own power and position and overestimate the capacity of connection to another) but to understand it as a disciplined effort to fully consider who the individuals are and the social conditions of which they are the product—that is, what has formed them as social animals. This is difficult intellectual work that requires "an attentiveness to the other and a self-abnegation and openness rarely encountered in everyday life."[45] It is a "*spiritual exercise* that, through *forgetfulness of self*, aims at a true *conversion of the way we look at* other people in the ordinary circumstances of life."[46]

Part of the work of forgetfulness of self and conversion to the other entails the disciplines of listening well; crafting careful, open-ended questions; offering assurances of care and confidentiality; and putting people at ease in every way possible. It also means study of the "social conditions of which they are a product" so that one can have an affinity for the unspoken social formations characterizing their life and circumstances.[47] It is, in technical terms, to have in mind all the dynamics of a particular field within which their particular *habitus* is formed. It is attentiveness to the world in the person in order to listen well to the person's being in the world.

43. Bourdieu et al., *The Weight of the World: Social Suffering in Contemporary Society*, trans. Priscilla Parkhurst Ferguson (Stanford, CA: Stanford University Press, 1999), 612.
44. Ibid., 614.
45. Ibid.
46. Ibid., emphasis original.
47. Ibid., 613.

When this happens, Bourdieu says, an interviewee can feel and experience the interview as an opportunity for "extraordinary discourse" that might never have been spoken but was already there, merely awaiting the conditions for its actualization. People often will take this situation as an opportunity "to testify, to make themselves heard, to carry their experience over from the private into the public sphere."[48] It even happens that the interview is taken over by the respondents, who in a way find the experience of really being heard to be "simultaneously gratifying and painful."[49] Sometimes, in witnessing a life in the self-forgetting of this exercise in understanding, "the most important thing is to silently wait."[50] Here, in the holy moment of deep silence, listening to another find words for the experiences of his or her life—lovely or horrible or more likely some mixture of both—the whole practice of research is subsumed by our participation in listening as God does, the God who bends near to hear our cries.[51]

48. Ibid., 615.
49. Ibid.
50. Ibid.
51. The theology of silence in relation to the craft of research is developed in Eileen Campbell-Reed and Christian Scharen, "Ethnography on Holy Ground: How Qualitative Interviewing Is Practical Theological Work," *International Journal of Practical Theology* 17, no. 2 (November 2013): 232–59.

Index